Degrees of Fidelity

For George who keeps us all [to]gether! — Steve

Degrees of Fidelity

*Essays on Poetry
and the Latitudes of the Personal*

In friendship

STEPHEN DUNN

TIGER BARK PRESS ❂ ROCHESTER, NEW YORK ❂ 2018

Published by Tiger Bark Press,
202 Mildorf Ave., Rochester, NY 14609.

Tiger Bark Press books are published by Steven Huff,
and designed by Philip Memmer.

Cover artwork by Rosalind Brenner.

Author photo by Nina Soifer.

ISBN-13: 978-1-7329012-0-9

This book made possible by the New York State Council on the Arts,
with the support of Governor Andrew M. Cuomo
and the New York State Legislature.

For James Hollis

Also by Stephen Dunn

POETRY

Whereas
Lines of Defense
Here and Now
What Goes On: Selected Poems 1995-2009
Everything Else in the World
The Insistence of Beauty
Local Visitations
Different Hours
Loosestrife
New and Selected Poems 1974-1994
Landscape at the End of the Century
Between Angels
Local Time
Not Dancing
Work and Love
Circus of Needs
Full of Lust and Good Usage
Looking for Holes in the Ceiling

PROSE

Walking Light: Essays and Memoirs
Riffs and Reciprocities

CHAPBOOKS

Five Impersonations
Winter at the Caspian Sea (with Lawrence Raab)
Falling Backwards into the World
Keeper of Limits: The Mrs. Cavendish Poems

BOOKS ABOUT

The Room and the World: Essays on the Poet Stephen Dunn
(edited by Laura McCullough)

Contents

Introduction

THERE COMES A TIME IN A POET'S DEVELOPMENT as a writer and as a reader when he or she is more interested in how a poem gets from here to there, and in what formal decisions have been made to achieve this or that effect, than in what the poem means. Or in locating the crossroad moment or moments when a poem could have gone one way, but instead was taken another way, which led to the rightness of a discovery. Such attention will eventually take us to meaning, if meaning is what we're after. But increasingly I'm interested in knowing where I am in a poem (physically and/or psychologically) so that I have a solid place from which to measure progress. The leap from nowhere to somewhere is thrilling if it leads to an unforeseen *thereness*, but if it shows no signs of moving toward the consequential it will likely have a short-term, first-effect-only-effect dazzle.

The poems to which I'm most drawn deliver the here and now of our existence while being inherently philosophical. If they wander from where they began, as they often do, I know from whence they came, and perhaps how their concealments are connected to their revelations. I want them to engage the heart and the mind simultaneously, and if they move us, it's not necessarily to tears. This book attempts to investigate where we are, how we got there, and where we might arrive if we make the moves that point the way.

Several of these essays deal with what I'd call the mysteries of composition, beginning with "Little Craft Manifesto" and including, among others, "The Poem, Its Buried Subject, and the Revisionist Reader." Some essays were motivated by the need to give a craft talk of my choosing at a writers' conference. Others were self-generated, arising from issues unresolved. The writing of these became for me acts of clarification, ways of finding out what I thought. Still others resulted from various quarrels with myself, quarrels with others, and quarrels with the culture. The latter produced speculation about what was behind misused words, for example "sucks" in "George Orwell Sucks," and about why men speak as they do to other men in "Locker Room Talk."

Other pieces lean toward memoir, subsequently revised from their original incarnations, or were given as talks in response to special occasions, for instance being inducted into the International Scholar/Athlete Hall of Fame, or being chosen as Alumnus of the Year by Hofstra University—opportunities that permitted me to muse on the relationship between sports and art, and on the value of a liberal education. Alongside those are various attempts to account for how I've become what I've become, which inevitably deal with the difficulties of telling the truth, and being "honest" in general.

Throughout, there is mention or analysis of writers and artists who have been influential, or whose work has compelled me to respond: Wallace Stevens, Franz Kafka, Samuel Beckett, Carson McCullers, H.L. Mencken. Wisława Szymborska, Jean Valentine, Donald Justice, Albert Camus, Marianne Moore, Fernando Pessoa, Robert Frost, Philip Larkin, Brigit Pegeen Kelly, Gerard Manley Hopkins, Sylvia Plath, Theodore Roethke, Louise Glück. E.A. Robinson, Jane Hirshfield, Lawrence Raab, Russell Edson, among a host of others—I am indebted to all of them.

This volume follows *Walking Light: Memoirs and Essays* (published by Norton in 1993 and reissued by BOA Editions in 2002, a book that attempted to explore issues of poetics while here and there ruminating about aspects of a life that had brought about such concerns. *Degrees of Fidelity* continues to explore these preoccupations, but I'd like to think with different emphases and an enlarged sense of how poems are made.

1

Little Craft Manifesto

CRAFT, IN THE BROADEST SENSE, IS A KIND OF PRESSURE that the poet puts on material in order to see what it can bear. The primary aim of craft is paradoxical—to exclude and accommodate. Craft wants to make room, for example, for odd companions, such as an etherized patient and a sky. But craft is an assassin to the extra word, or any failure of precision. Ear and eye do its work, if they've been properly trained. Logic and emotional intelligence are among its adjudicators, if for no other reason than they have experience with breaking down. A good mind helps, if it contains at least a small library and is not in love with itself.

Craft is an act of, as much a disciplining of, discoveries and excitements, as it can be a permission for wildness to be wild, subtlety to be subtle. In fact, craft usually involves many acts, and is evidence—draft by draft—of the poet finding his way. Craft is an orchestration of words and desired effects. Essentially, its job is to reveal content. It's in the business of heightening, subordinating, pacing. It controls rates of disclosure, degrees of importance; it manages tone. Like a compass, it's what you need when you're lost, but it is not sufficient.

It will not help the uninteresting, the cowardly, or anyone wishing to save the world. Craft is most kind to those who've spent long hours worrying about it—the problem solvers, those who are suspicious of the satisfactory. It is especially fond of poets who understand that a good poem is not only difficult to write, but unlikely, as well as poets who've written enough to know some of its secrets—one of which is that passion and aesthetic distance can be compatible, that one without the other often results in noise or mere scaffolding. Craft has a curious integrity; it doesn't want only to be itself.

If you're a serious poet, every poem you write is part of a long unspoken dialogue with the poets who preceded you. Craft is part of that dialogue, preferably unspoken. As you write, you need not be conscious of your forebears and their work, but the poem should in some way reflect that you've absorbed their contributions. The new always owes a debt to the old. If, for example, how to successfully manage a conceit intrigues you, best that you know some of its good ghosts, perhaps starting with Donne, and have acquainted yourself with its difficulties. When it comes to making metaphors, there's a very thin line between virtuosity and tripping over into indulgence. One of the common errors of the fledgling poet is a reflexive love of the extended metaphor. Metaphors shouldn't be cranked up. They should arise out of necessity. They should be reached for when something crucial can't be said straight out, when only analogue will do. Extended metaphor, in the wrong hands, is faux poetry. Much can happen, though, when you realize you've boxed yourself in, that your extended metaphor is more a prison than an opportunity to be ingenious. How liberating then to abandon it, or to relax it, to let the poem find its own limits. To have a sense of such things is an aspect of craft.

Craft, of course, needs something of substance to work with, and the poets' hardest work may come once their "subject" has been intuited or arrived at, and they have a sense of what their principle of selection is. This can happen at any stage of composition, but when it does the poet is at a dangerous juncture. How not to become too purposeful? How to keep composing with the same verve as when you were in aimless flight, one detail finding the next? Here's what I try to remember when I've reached that moment of consciousness: Once you arrive at your subject, you no longer need to be committed to it. Instead, you should resist those details that readily come to mind. If, for example, you discover that you're writing about the horrors of war, you'll want to avoid words like "carnage" or "bloody," language that too easily attaches itself to the subject. Or you'll want to use those very words and redeem them.

Subject matter is best thought of as an occasion you've provided to yourself so that you might be interesting. If you're not startled by your own claims or phrasing, no one else will be. Rethink them. This is how you might free yourself from the banalities of the known, the long yawn of the easy. Charles Olson's dictum is useful here: "One perception must immediately lead to another perception." Properly understood, it should help get you to where you haven't been. But then it will be useful to veer away from its perceptions, or at least doubt them as absolutes, else your poem become frenetic. Craft often has something to do with modulation, often too with expansion.

Craft can accommodate the exotic, shape a place for the loose-ended. It is nothing if not an agent of the possible. And yet your goal is to reach the stage where craft is a nonissue, where all of the above is so much a part of your wherewithal that you don't have to think about it.

This might take years. In the meantime, craft will seem like making the right decision at the crossroads. You'll feel that to go one way, or to go the other way, is important, and it is. But really what matters is how interesting you can make either journey. There's no right decision. In one direction, let's say there's a party. In the other, a descent into despair. Yet there's always at least a third choice, that road perhaps duller than the others, devoid of high spirits and despair's strange glamor. And it might be your best choice, so in need will it be of imagination. You won't know for sure until you get to the end of it. And actually the decision need not constitute high drama. This isn't life we're talking about. In poetry, there's no reason why all of these roads can't be traveled.

Degrees of Fidelity

SEVERAL YEARS AGO IN AN ESSAY, I found myself invoking Robert Frost's insight, "We shall be known by the delicacy of where we stop short." I tried to use it as a standard that would resonate into my dealings with others, especially those closest to me, and into matters of aesthetics. What we choose not to do in a poem, for example, may reveal as much about us as what we choose to include. This seems particularly so if our subject involves family.

Yet, as poets, our fidelity to people we know is always complicated by our fidelities to the poem and the language we find ourselves using, not to mention what we consider to be the truth itself. While in many instances our subjects will be served by restraint, we can imagine, in other instances, that they might be served by extravagance, a going beyond proprieties and conventions. By the end of my essay, I found myself embracing Frost's statement *and* arguing for a poetry of uncommon, surpassing gestures. I don't think one necessarily excludes the other.

Nevertheless, poems—restrained or extravagant or some combination of the two—that involve or implicate family members should raise certain questions for those of us who write them. Why are we writing about this particular subject in the first place? Certainly we have the entire world of experience to draw from. Why this poem about brother, or mother? Why now? And what must such a poem do to involve strangers in what's personal to us? As the cry of its own occasion, a worthy poem ideally should suggest some answers to those questions.

My experience as both a writer and a reader has convinced me that most poems about family should be put in a locked cabinet, kept, if kept at all, as private data for our children to find after we're dead. Some family poems, however, driven by necessity and in search of the elusive properties of their subjects, deserve the light of day. For them to merit this, their authors will have needed to develop new allegiances—to texture, tone, rhythm, to name just a few—as the poem evolved. If not, there'll be Trouble with a capital T in Poetry City. Beware the poet who values content more than the handling of content, a danger especially present in our most personal poems.

If poems about family are always going to involve some degree of personal disclosure, how that disclosure is tonally delivered, not to mention paced and framed, usually will determine its success. Sylvia Plath's "Daddy" is interesting to examine in this regard. It is clearly a poem of extravagance but not without discipline. Whatever we might think of its claims, it's clear that Plath had as much allegiance to sound pattern, rhythm, and overall orchestration of effects as she did to indicting her father. It's an amazingly vitriolic performance. Despite her bile, she remained committed to the poem as a poem, a made thing, a system of words and sounds. This is a poem, though, that never confronts itself and that always asserts rather than explores. Yet only because of biographical reasons do we question its tone. If we were ignorant of her biography, we would simply accept it as a poem of rage. Plath was burdened by the psychological weight of her perceived victimization but, of course, didn't have to worry that the victimizer might see her poem. He was long dead. The poem reads like an exorcism and she, no doubt, found a kind of radical freedom in its composition, a freedom achieved at high cost. We can be sure that she was also liberated, paradoxically, by what was at the heart of her poem's complaint: her father's absence.

The dead free us as much as the living constrain us. But constraint, I would argue, is often useful. The need to suppress can be an impetus to transformation, to ingenuity, to the virtues of indirection. Think of how the dramatic structure in "Home Burial" gave Frost permission to examine and explore the alienation in a particular marriage. He must have felt that he needed such a construct (tantamount to a mask) to engage what was personal to him. Or think how Theodore Roethke's rhymes and iambic trimeter in "My Papa's Waltz" helped create a tone that lightened what otherwise might be construed as an indictment of a father's violence. Roethke's fidelity to form, we can say, kept the extravagance of emotions in check. We should consider it our good fortune that many poets have been unable or have chosen not to address their subjects directly.

I know someone who is able to write about his adulteries because, he says, his wife is not interested in reading his poems. (Some would consider this a good reason for adultery.) Yet I'm not sure that the freedom he feels necessarily makes for better poetry. It seems like a sad, not a radical, freedom, insufficiently hard won. Most of us are cognizant that the poem we write which implicates or involves our spouses or significant others will constitute a matter of delicacy. If, at a certain time in our lives, that sort of poem insists on itself, becomes necessary subject matter, then so be it. If handled more or less directly, we'll need to seek tactics that will permit us to go far enough so that we understand what stopping short might mean. Maybe we'll pretend we're a flower, as Louise Glück so marvelously did in *The Wild Iris*. Or find a strategy like Berryman's in his *Dream Songs*, where competing voices and rarefied syntax blur the purely autobiographical. Artifice can not only save poems but, perhaps, marriages as well. The too naked poem, one that makes dirty laundry its flag and never gets beyond its original impulse, is a poem we have failed. We should hide it from everyone.

Is a poem ever worth the discomfort or embarrassment of, say, the family member it alludes to or discusses? Many poets have thought so, especially since the advent of so-called confessional poetry in the late 1950s. My loosely held rule is that if my poem has found ways to discover and explore its subject, if it has on balance become more of a fictive than a confessional act, then—regardless of its connotations—I will not be discomfited or embarrassed by it. But to raise the notion of the fictive is also to raise corollary questions. What, if anything, would we falsify, say, about our mothers for the sake of being interesting? Do family stories, written in the first person, make a covenant with the reader that implies a fidelity to the actual? If they were written in the third person, would that covenant change somewhat? Put crudely, how many among us would exploit our grandmothers for an exquisite stanza? We know that Plath's father, for example, was not a Nazi. But no one knows for sure whether my mother, in fact, obliged me after I requested to see her breasts when I was twelve, as I claim she did in my poem "The Routine Things Around the House."

When Mother died
I thought: now I'll have a death poem.
That was unforgivable

yet I've since forgiven myself
as sons are able to do
who've been loved by their mothers.

I stared into the coffin
knowing how long she'd live,
how many lifetimes there are

in the sweet revisions of memory.
It's hard to know exactly
how we ease ourselves back from sadness,

but I remembered when I was twelve,
1951, before the world
unbuttoned its blouse.

I had asked my mother (I was trembling)
if I could see her breasts
and she took me into her room

without embarrassment or coyness
and I stared at them,
afraid to ask for more.

Now, years later, someone tells me
Cancers who've never had mother love
are doomed and I, a Cancer,

feel blessed again. What luck
to have had a mother
who showed me her breasts

when girls my age were developing
their separate countries,
what luck

she didn't doom me
with too much or too little.
Had I asked to touch,

perhaps to suck them,
what would she have done?
Mother, dead woman

who I think permits me
to love women easily,
this poem

is dedicated to where
we stopped, to the incompleteness
that was sufficient

and how you buttoned up,
began doing the routine things
around the house.

I tell you here that she did show me her breasts. Would I have
written so if she hadn't? I don't think I would have. I think, though, there
are details that I made up. I've lived so long with the way I mythologized
the event that I can't remember which ones are which. But I do remember
feeling, after much revision, that all the details, fictive or actual, contributed
to the poem's emotional veracity.

The truth is that for many years the poem made me uncomfortable;
to mishandle such subject matter was to descend into the vulgar. When
I was finally able to get myself to include it in a book, it was because I'd
discovered its hidden subject. The poem was not just a provocative personal
story about a mother's grace under pressure, as I had thought, but it was also

about limits. The way she showed me her breasts and then buttoned up had taught me something important about when and how to stop short.

There are degrees of fidelity to the actual. I don't know a single poet who would hesitate at locating, say, a spousal argument in Paramus instead of Princeton if that change better served the poem's sonics. Although some family matters and memories should, I suppose, be sacrosanct, very few, even with the best of intentions, are immutable. In essence, they are emotionally incomplete without the stories that shape and subjectify them. Large events in our lives especially have a para-factual existence. When we start talking about them, we are already changing them.

We will be known by our track record. If we hold nothing dear, that will show and indict us over time. If our falsifications and embellishments, in large part, serve the genuine and the true, that, too, will show over time. If we are restrained when our emotional stakes are already small, we have misused restraint. If our extravagances are more glitter than substance, we probably should have found more ways to contain and constrain. Finally, the writer's worst sin is to be uninteresting. I wouldn't kill off my grandmother for an exquisite stanza, but I'd certainly travel with her to Bolivia, where we never went, or rescue her from her inveterate silence, if setting and speech could bring her alive.

A State of Disunion

Some Thoughts on Poetry, History, As if, and No

WE ADMIRE THE PEOPLE WHO TRY TO MAKE THINGS HAPPEN, effect change, especially those who work against injustice. But as much as they remain significant, one wonders if effectiveness will often sacrifice truth for the realization of its goals. The well-told partial truth, Spalding Gray says, deflects the raw truth beneath it. Those of us who write know how easy it is to hide behind felicities. We also know that to suppress is not necessarily a bad thing; it can lead to transformation, the need to find another way of saying something.

I plan to ease in to what you've asked me to talk about tonight, to find my way as I go, deliberately seeking detours as a way of speculating on or worrying about new scenery, and about some of the bad neighborhoods of contemporary poetry. Forgive me if I start with a movie.

On the advice of some friends, I watched *I Am*, a documentary made by former Hollywood comedy director Tom Shadyac about how to improve the world. Like many utopian notions, I prefer Camus' idea of a "relative utopia," which he defined as a philosophy free of all messianic elements, and devoid of nostalgia for an earthly paradise. The thinking behind Shadyac's film remained annoyingly ahistorical throughout, with just token depictions of war and rallies against it, civil rights marches, and such. Occasionally, we'd see Nazis mechanistically parading, all this without commentary by the voice-over. The voice-over at other moments would recommend that we love each other, do good deeds, and so on.

Periodically, the movie gave us excerpts from interviews with some genuine heroes from the past century—Martin Luther King, Nelson Mandela, Howard Zinn, Mahatma Gandhi, Desmond Tutu—to support its viewpoint. No mention of Hitler or Stalin or Mao. Not once is the word evil mentioned, not once were great writers like Sophocles, Hawthorne, or Melville evoked or discussed. In Shadyac's view, the human heart was devoid of darkness. And we were presented scientific evidence from the natural world that all things are interconnected, from which only positive conclusions were drawn.

The movie made me long for Hobbes and Marx and Nietzsche, for analyses of history and human nature that run counter to the documentary's viewpoint, or at least acknowledge that other world views exist. The people I've mentioned above are emblems of vision and bravery because they are the exceptions. Each effected important changes, and all were able to inspire large movements. Yet the same could be said of Hitler and Mao. They too believed they were improving the world.

They were wrong, of course. But what they did tended to perversely support the movie's main contention: that in essence our natures are fundamentally cooperative, we're driven to get along, not to dominate, the will toward good is stronger than the will to power. What the movie never brought up was that the will to do good is always a tyrant's appeal. (The world will be a better place if we purify it of differences. Let's all be equal. Let's kill the property owners and share the land.) Shadyac would have us ignore mass graves, religious zealotry, the dangers of the true believer. It takes a lot of folks joining together, cooperating with each other, to wage war.

During the movie, somebody asks the Dalai Lama what the world most needs. He says "critical thinking," which the movie proceeds to ignore. Good thinking, it seems to me, involves saying no before saying yes; that is, to hold out for the more satisfactory yes. Then maybe doubt that one, too. This means a constant measuring against notions that have preceded it, which means Euclid gives way to Einstein; the world according to Genesis yields to the world according to Darwin; and, in a different sense of influence, Whitman opens the way for Ginsberg.

If poets improve the world—and we must not write with that intention—we do so gradually, over time.

We do it by precisions, corrections. A visionary is someone who sees the unseen interconnections, identifies them, gives them accuracy's radiance. The visionary is someone who sees the present as it is. The visionary, for my purposes here, is the poet. The poet lets into the poem the strange, the unmanageable, and tries to create a livable environment for them. The result need not be pretty. What's beautiful in a poem, for me, is often a balancing act of factors—the ugly, say, under a sunset—the stuff of the world delivered in its variety and complexity.

In Robert Frost's essay/Introduction to Edwin Arlington Robinson's *King Jasper*, ". . . content with the old-fashioned way to be new," he recounts a conversation he had with a young man who says, "Whereas we once thought literature should be without content, we now know it should be charged full of propaganda." Wrong twice, Frost says to him. But the young man pushes his case: "Surely art can be considered good only as it prompts to action." How soon? Frost replies, and goes on to say, "We must be very tender of our dreamers." And then, "We shan't mind what they seem, if only they produce real poems."

To register what it feels like to be alive in a particular moment in history is an enormous task. The poets who aspire to do so instruct us in various ways. But there are many other ends apart from instruction to which poets aspire. Some will seek to dazzle, to make words sing and startle. Others will want to oppose the aesthetic that preceded them. Valéry wanted poetry to be a holiday of the mind. I'd like to make my imagination yours. Great poets, I suppose, like Shakespeare, Dickinson, Stevens (we each can make our own lists) will aspire to all of the above.

Most of us who write know that the genuine can emerge from the arbitrary, seriousness from play, profundity from resistance. Most of us know that poems *should* get away from us. We long to feel like we're flying, or on fire, have gotten beyond our original intention. My compositional pleasures involve giving myself permission to say what I've found myself saying. Completing a poem is often a matter of stitching and arranging, of rewriting line two to make sense of that startling wildness you found yourself writing in line eighteen. The purpose behind such stitching and rearranging should be veracity, with the goal of moving the reader to a different sense of regard.

Frost again: "Practice of an art is more salutary than talk about it. There is nothing more composing than composition."

Suddenly, or so it seemed to me, we found ourselves in the era of French criticism, and the unreading of literature. And a lot of bad poetry. We learned how to deconstruct, which was valuable. To construct anew was a different matter. Poems written out of theoretical conviction, I came to feel, will likely read that way.

Most poems driven by a postmodern sense of language's indeterminacy are, at best, merely interesting. The poets who bought in to the (albeit correct) notion that language is comprised of signifiers seemed to feel that they didn't have to try very hard to make sense. What was the point? This could be substituted for that, that for this. But if language is indeterminate, it seems we should have all the more reason to work hard to make it yield sense.

As for my own use of language in a poem, my approach didn't change much. I kept revising it, attempting to give it some music so it would at least give the illusion of behaving for a while. And my habit was to sufficiently distrust what I wrote until it could be shaped into consequence. But the author was dead, which some people believed, and texts were read as evidence of social and political currents. *Texts.* That's what our poems were called. Dry things by dead people, fit for autopsies.

"For poetry makes nothing happen," writes W.H. Auden in his elegy for Yeats. The quotation is often left at that. To be fair to Auden's meaning, it shouldn't be. The sentence continues,

> it survives
> In the valley of its saying where executives
> Would never want to tamper; it flows south
> From ranches of isolation and the busy griefs,
> Raw towns that we believe and die in; it survives,
> a way of happening, a mouth.

It's a way of happening, it resides beneath most consciousness. It survives, even for those not disposed to it, subliminally. To accomplish this, sometimes we need to be unreasonable. All of our great heroes were unreasonable in the face of powers that defined what was reasonable. If asked, they probably wouldn't claim heroism for themselves. They might say their motive was unhappiness. Or a consciousness they couldn't deny once they had it. Or justice.

The *I Am* movie perpetuates sweet lies. It possessed all the dangers of naiveté delivered with sincerity and earnestness. One issue that the movie raises is, Can one offer truths that don't engage with their opposites? I'm not sure of the answer to that, but I do feel, along with Joseph Brodsky, that evil "tends to appear in the guise of good," and that "nothing can be turned and worn inside out with greater ease than one's notion of social justice, civic conscience, a better future, etc." To get the world right is not necessarily a sanguine act.

As if thinking liberates the possible. Moral certainties confine the possible. It seems to me that a good poem might employ a combination of such thinking. A student of mine wrote, "Left by Fate at the altar years ago, Lust had an ax to grind." "As if her Lust had an ax to grind" would make the line more plausible, I told her, though nothing could save "ax to grind." Moral certainty may exclude flights of imagination, and at the same time be an invitation to ingenuity, just as strict form can be. Compelled by assignment to write a love sonnet about a failed relationship in which the moon somehow would be involved, another student completed his poem with this couplet—

> I gave you a diamond. It should have been a pearl.
> It should have been a stone to hang above the world.

—a loveliness, I think, that couldn't be arrived at without the constraints he freely accepted. The *I Am* movie put little in the way of its original position, so never underwent the pressure that leads to discovery. Nor did the film need any *as ifs* because it rarely risked saying anything outrageous or exotic.

In a poem, I want to behave *as if* what I say matters, even though few are listening. That means trying to be as clear as possible, which doesn't obviate difficulty. We say what we can straight out until we no longer can. At some point we must reach for analogue to approximate what we're after. We move into the possibly murky, possibly crystalizing, world of metaphor. But we must not be wholly happy to be there, nor by our moments of apt phrasing. We need to know that a poem is the sum of its effects, and that sum is a metaphor too. If a poem's surfaces are compelling, good readers don't mind difficulty. I don't. But I also don't seek it. Deliberate obfuscators I think are cowardly, afraid to enter the world of sense, and the possibilities of failure.

Saints and radicals wish to go all the way. We love and admire them for how far they're willing to go. But they frighten us, ask us to be better than ourselves. However, when it comes to writing poetry the single-mindedness they bring with them is a hindrance. Ambivalence makes one hesitate, reconsider. It's the enemy of action, and a staple of the poet who lives in the fuzzy world he'd like to plumb and assay. (The poet's test of bravery arises in repressive countries where poets are taken seriously—think of Osip Mandelstam, think of Nâzim Hikmet, et al.) My guess is that they wrote out of the same motives some poets in the U.S. do—to make sense of their world, or out of anger and a sense of injustice. Their personal is political. Their bravery is to publish.

They take their place alongside the Mandelas and the Gandhis of the world. It's a lie to say that slogans like "Love one another" could save anyone from the crazies out there. But to behave toward each other as if love mattered is a notion I say a guarded yes to.

I came of age twice, once in the passive late fifties, the Eisenhower years. Again in the late sixties, in graduate school. amid drugs and rock 'n' roll, sex, politics, protest marches. Watching *I Am*, I had no feeling for its depiction of the fifties, but some for the sixties. Yet the movie also reflected our self-righteousness, our frequent stupidities in the name of progress and high-mindedness. The movie made few distinctions. It congratulated its maker on changing his life, and a generation on being itself.

Yet it brought back a sexy, heady time—Dylan replacing Pat Boone. Richie Havens erasing *Leave It to Beaver*. I started to long for words that helped define my experience. I had memorized Roethke's "In a Dark Time." His "Which I is I?" made me feel sane, not confused. William Meredith, in his poem "The Cheer," wrote, ". . . the cheer, reader my friend, is in the words here, somewhere" and I kept looking for it. Some of us dared to speak of our souls, and about the unspeakable. The surreal infused the real. Absurdity became a kind of clarity. For proof, all we had to do was read the headlines.

And Russell Edson's nuttiness made perfect sense, as did Bill Knott's peculiarities. Samuel Beckett, too, regularly came to the rescue. The tragic world was funny. And was not.

In the postmodern climate (that I hope is fading into the past), all assertions seemed to have quotation marks around them. Multicultural work was valuable regardless of its value. Critical thinking was what you did after you read a few critics. Nobody would go to the wall for what they believed, or would acknowledge the importance of feeling. Of course I'm exaggerating. In among the blurring and the invention for invention's sake, John Ashbery, for one, was gradually teaching us how to read him, as Stevens had a few generations earlier. His fractured narratives, his refusals to give us what we wanted, were borne out of a way of seeing, a world view. It wasn't his fault that most of his imitators loved obfuscation more than they did poetry. The poetry world was in need of its Clement Greenberg or its Randall Jarrell. Instead we got William Logan (whose bile always seems to get in the way of both his critical stances and his praise).

Surely there's nothing wrong with experimentation. It can show the way. The problem is how long we usually have to wait for the genius to emerge, employing the same techniques with a compelling and justifying newness. Greenberg helped to identify for us the Pollocks and the Klees. His comment about certain experimental art—"all surprise without satisfaction" could easily apply to any art that's trying too hard to be new. Robert Frost wasn't attempting to be experimental, but Jarrell and Lionel Trilling articulated new ways of understanding him. How many artists are waiting for the right critic to identify their worth?

Well, I began this ramble by invoking a film, and I seem to be ending it by mostly invoking painters and art critics. While loving the wildness and play of Pollack and Klee, I'll conclude with a prejudice that I share with a different, but no less excellent artist, Edward Hopper. Think poetry as I quote it. Hopper said that "Painting will have to deal more fully and less obliquely with life and nature's phenomena before it can again become great."

Frost again: "We shan't mind [the experimenters] . . . if only they produce real poems."

The Poem, Its Buried Subject, and the Revisionist Reader

Behind the Composition of "The Guardian Angel"

TO REVISIT AN OLD POEM OF YOUR OWN is often to come to it as an interested stranger. With time having passed, you're more reader than author, and like any reader you bring to the poem an aesthetic and a psychology forged by personal history and a history of reading. If twenty years have elapsed since you've written a poem about a certain kind of spiritual endurance, and in the meantime you've become, say, a communist, and have turned almost exclusively to reading poems for their political significance, then you're likely that poem's revisionist reader. Even if your outlook has remained roughly the same, the world around you hasn't, and will inevitably provide you with a different angle of regard. The good reader works hard at trying to compensate for these occurrences, tries to give each poem a fair trial and a fair sentence, but the writer as reader of his own poem may still be clinging—perhaps even rightly so—to some old allegiances. But one thing is sure: As author, no matter how well you've blended your intentions with your discoveries, the reader always completes your poem.

At first, I found this intolerable, like someone else renaming my child. And, I confess, it remains intolerable much of the time. But. So much that's instructive begins with *but*. Moreover, if I agree with the novelist Stendhal, and I do, "that speech was given to man to conceal his thoughts," then I shouldn't have been very much surprised that my poem "The Guardian Angel," or any poem, for that matter, might have an elusive subtext. But I was surprised.

No, I hadn't become a communist. However, twenty years did elapse before I revisited "The Guardian Angel," enough time for me to witness the poem differently. Almost instantly, there it was—the buried subject—hiding like much of the world itself, not far from the surface.

More often than not, to be wholly unaware of what's driving your poem means that you're listening to the wrong cues, and therefore likely to make poor choices. You think you're writing about *that time she left me*, but fail to realize that your poem might simultaneously need to be exploring the nature of loss. You're following the lesser drift. You need to revise, but as long as the deeper subject remains hidden you're only thinking cosmetically, just shifting a few words around. Or, what you allow yourself to think of as subtlety is really just a kind of avoidance, an unconscious refusal to enter certain delicate territory. Or, even more typically these days, you're in the headlong process of composing associatively, disparate image following disparate image, but never seem to arrive at the poem's locus of concern. You're dazzling, you're on your way to postmodernist heaven, but you've yet to find a principle of selection; almost anything can be substituted for anything else. The radical entry into your subject eludes you. Your poem has taken its place among the many casualties of indulgent unconsciousness.

Here's the paradox. Successful poems are often written with a comparable unconsciousness. Buried subjects, even when they are the products of inattention or avoidance, can give poems a behind-the-scenes radiance. "The Guardian Angel," I'm quite sure, is one of those poems that profited by what I didn't know about it. What follows—this retrospective foray into the making of a poem—will be a re-creation, thus a fiction, which is to say I'm interested in approximating the truth. With luck, this rereading will live as the poem's good companion, casting some light and maybe a few shadows.

Trust the tale, not the teller, D.H. Lawrence admonishes. I'm aware of such wisdom. *But.* But, on the other hand, let me say that I wish for you to trust everything I say, although admittedly I'm not without guile or strategy. Here is the poem:

The Guardian Angel

Afloat between lives and stale truths
   he realizes
he's never truly protected one soul,

they all die anyway, and what good
   is solace,
solace is cheap. The signs are clear:

the drooping wings, the shameless thinking
    about utility
and self. It's time to stop.

The guardian angel lives for a month
    with other angels,
sings the angelic songs, is reminded

that he doesn't have a human choice.
    The angel of love
lies down with him, and loving

restores to him his pure heart.
    Yet how hard it is
to descend into sadness once more.

When the poor are evicted, he stands
    between them
and the bank, but the bank sees nothing

in its way. When the meek are overpowered
    he's there, the thin air
through which they fall. Without effect

he keeps getting in the way of insults.
    He keeps wrapping
his wings around those in the cold.

Even his lamentations are unheard,
    though now,
in for the long haul, trying to live

beyond despair, he believes, he needs
    to believe
everything he does takes root, hums

beneath the surfaces of the world.

I like to talk about the composition of poems as involving a series of allegiances that we keep as long as we can, but which we modify and refine as the language we employ starts to make its own demands. In "The Guardian Angel," my initial allegiance was to creating a secular angel, an allegiance I gradually abandoned. Instead, I found myself with a disaffected guardian angel, the poem's first real discovery. I vaguely remember discarding all the language and claims (two or three stanzas worth of warm-up) that had gotten me to that discovery, instead beginning right away with his disaffectedness. "Afloat between lives and stale truths, / he realizes / he's never truly protected one soul." I was in a "what if" poem. What if there was such a thing as a disaffected angel? How would he act? What would he be thinking? I had two allegiances now, to the serious playfulness of executing his disaffection, and to finding an imaginative logic for it. A drama was unfolding. He was, by definition, a do-gooder, one who now was thinking only of self. Worse, he was thinking of results, as if he could be the arbiter of what a result was. Wasn't that for Someone else to decide? I was starting to become interested in him. But only in him. I had no idea that something else might also be driving the poem.

I suppose the next lines became available to me because I was at a writers' colony. The angel seeks out his own kind, and is restored by them, especially by the angel of love who, by example, is able to remind him of generosity and its worth. Prior to these moments, my compositional possibilities were wide open. Now I had narrowed them by choosing to have him healed. He might have been an interesting renegade, confrontational and subversive, disruptive of the established order. He might have wanted a new identity, a job that required less of him. I'm sure I could have written in either of those directions as well as in others. We learn, as Roethke says, by going where we go.

I can't remember if, around this time, I knew that I was taking my angel on a rather classical religious journey—that he would lose his way before he found his way, that some kind of passage was being enacted. This was apparent to me later. What I did know at the time was that play had gotten me beyond the purely fanciful; that is, beyond the pleasures of invention, beyond the poem as exercise. I had arrived at some principle of selection, which could help me find the poem's next moments: the guardian angel would not quit, that wasn't one of his choices. Nevertheless, I recognized how difficult it would be for him "to descend into sadness once more." I only half-knew where I was going, and therefore could still avoid the perils of purposefulness, could ride some uncodified energy. In retrospect, these were my new allegiances: to the poem's adjusted original impulse; to the texture, sounds, and rhythms of the language used so far; and to the unknowns of this new, governing drift.

I wasn't conscious of needing to come up with a series of tests for his new-found resolve, but that's what I found myself doing. Okay, he returns to earth and to his job. What's likely to be his experience? Certainly, if the poem were to stay in the realm of the probable, he would once again fail. But I was as much committed to the poem's rhythmical recurrences as I was to the recurrences of his ineffectuality, and I may have known there couldn't be the latter without the former. I had begun to feel for him, and the rhythm had to authenticate this. Which is to say that content decisions were inseparable from decisions about syntax and flow, and were just a part of the overall orchestration of effects. Earlier, perhaps, I could have let content drive the poem, but no longer. Of course there were still various content options available to me. I could have allowed him, for example, one success. That would have set the poem on a slightly different course. In this case, what I ended up not selecting proved instructive. It, too, pointed the way.

The poem was leaning into its structure, though hadn't yet found its true form, if form, as Levertov says, is the revelation of content.

At the time I frequently used a step-down, three line stanza to harness and discipline my discursive inclinations. Initially, it was an editing device, to help identify and abolish excess content. This would evolve into a way of thinking about the poem as architecture. That is, as something that would seek its shape, stanza by stanza, by an acute attention to its inner relationships. Structurally, thus far, the poem had three movements: the introduction of the disaffected angel, his resurrection into new resolve, and his return to duty, which proved no more successful than before. Whatever mixture of intellection and obsession that was driving the poem was now calling for a fourth movement, and thus would take me toward the often illusory world of closure. The poet's temperament and compositional tics are always involved in that mysterious world, but since they're usually the last things we can do anything about, it's better instead to be as alert as possible to the poem's overt promptings. I tried to be. But by this time my choices, to a significant degree, were being made for me. I was both creator and responder to my creation. I'm not sure if I ever consciously chose to have the guardian angel live with his ineffectualness.

Nor did I ever consider having him quit again, which now seems a reasonable option. It just felt right, I suppose, to have him persevere in spite of repeated failure. At the moment, I knew I had moved him from disaffection, but to what? Acceptance? Resignation? A desperate hopefulness? Some instructive thread would need to be pulled through if closure were to take the poem to what could feel like its inevitability.

Well, that's one fiction, one way to speculate about what I found myself doing. Another, which will be even less coherent and therefore, I think, closer to the truth, is that the poem was composed during many sittings, had many false starts, much extraneous language, and stanzas in various orders. Parts of it, I vaguely recall, were cargoed in from other poems, those failed poems most of us save and steal from. I revised it over a period of months, and many of the revisions were arrived at, as I said before, because of the exigencies of rhythm and the seeking of cooperative sounds, determining what weight of language a stanza could bear, and other considerations that had more to do with problem-solving than with genesis or willfulness. At some point, that hint of a thread, that elusive something, famously invisible when the poem isn't on the right course, appeared. The angel, "in for the long haul," could not *not* be who he was. As it turns out, it was only a semblance of the real thread, but finding the ghost of it enabled me, I think, to create an illusion of orderliness and authority. Such a thread starts to become visible the more a poem's surface felicities get in some concordance with the pulse of its undercurrents.

Now, having said this, I recognize that from the start I was the god of this universe made of words, and had considerable time before book publication—cool, considered time—to assay and evaluate all of my choices, conscious and unconscious. I am responsible for everything in it, and could have, had I been foolishly or even perhaps wisely willful, changed its direction, pulled the thread through to a different conclusion, made the poem happier, sadder, etc. But my overriding allegiance was to the poem as a whole, to my fiction and its interlocking parts, and to how they held up for examination their revelations and concealments. Finally, we leave or abandon our poems because no more aesthetic decisions seem available to us that will help enact or explore our subject. At least I could think of none before "The Guardian Angel" found its way into my book *Between Angels*.

But "finally" is premature. Twenty years after the poem was written, I was visiting a colleague's class in which some of my poems were under discussion. She was, in fact, teaching *Between Angels*, and one of her students asked if I could read and comment on "The Guardian Angel." I hadn't read the poem in a while, and as I read it, it seemed clear to me what my buried subject had been. Was I seeing what was truly there, or was I bringing to an old poem new urgencies that somehow permitted them to be entertained? It's true, that at the time of the rereading, I had been preoccupied with the generation of poets in love with the romance of self-destruction, the generation of Berryman and Schwartz and Jarrell, and thinking about how few of them made it out of their fifties. And it's true that I had begun to wonder about myself in that regard. I remember smiling as I told the class that the poem is an analogue of the poet's condition in America. The poet does his job, I said, and hardly anybody listens or cares. All his life he lives with his ineffectuality, his invisible presence, the reality that there's little evidence that he makes anything happen. But

. . . trying to live

    beyond despair, he believes, he needs
      to believe,
    everything he does takes root, hums

    beneath the surfaces of the world.

There it was, my dogged optimism, my little anthem for continuing. This "what if" poem, this verbal construct that had found out just enough about itself to sustain the angel's journey from disaffection to endurance was a personal poem after all. The buried subject, I was sure now, had been the poem's co-driving force and its secret glue.

But wait. Even if what I just said is persuasive, there's another wrinkle. If the poem's hidden subject and the thread I pulled through are similar, as they now seem to have been, how can I have pulled through a thread I didn't become conscious of until years later? One answer, as I've suggested, is that the making of a poem is a constant compromise between author's intent and the discoveries that confound it. This process itself is a kind of decision maker, has its own intelligence, and is more alert to undercurrents than I could have been. Ultimately there's no answer, just more or less plausible fictions. Or I did it, I pulled the secret thread down and through while thinking only of the angel's problems and how to arrange them. Such things happen all the time, taking their places among the mysteries of composition.

Style

MANY YEARS AGO I WAS INTERVIEWED by Judith Kitchen and Stan Rubin for the Brockport Writers Forum. The focus was on my poem "Essay on the Personal," a poem that still holds up for me, but which now I would discuss somewhat differently. Rubin began by stating that the poem sets the personal against style in an interesting way, and I found myself trying to s speculate on whether that was true.

First the poem:

Because finally the personal
is all that matters,
we spend years describing stones,
chairs, abandoned farm houses—
until we're ready. Always
it's a matter of precision,
what it feels like
to kiss someone or to walk
out the door. How good it was
to practice on stones
which were things we could love
without weeping over. How good
someone else abandoned the farmhouse,
bankrupt and desperate.
Now we can bring a fine edge
to our parents. We can hold hurt
up to the sun for examination.
But just when we think we have it,
the personal goes the way of
belief. What seemed so deep
begins to seem naïve, something

that could be trusted
because we hadn't read Plato
or held two contradictory ideas
or women in the same day.
Love, then, becomes an old movie.
Loss seems so common
it belongs to the air,
to breath itself, anyone's.
We're left with style, a particular way
of standing and saying,
the idiosyncratic look
at the frown which means nothing
until we say it does. Years later,
long after we believed it peculiar
to ourselves, we return to love.
We return to everything
strange, inchoate, like living
with someone, like living alone,
settling for the partial, the almost
satisfactory sense of it.

I reiterated what I thought the poem was saying—that the experiential details of our lives are communal, that a poem's content is communal. Style is what's most individuating, thus most personal. It's how we speak about our experiences that distinguishes us from one another. And to achieve something like a style it might be wise to practice writing about things other than our lives, like stones and farmhouses. At the very least, our sensibilities would be apparent, maybe even our personalities, which Eliot had cautioned poets to subdue. (Good advice, I thought, only if you already have a personality.)

Style, I'd say now, is what gives élan to voice, enlarges it, gives it a recognizable spirit. It is what we expect to be present poem after poem. It is the infusion of sensibility, if not personality, into subject matter. Voice is its close cousin, but is likely to differ according to situation, whereas style permeates, and is generally more individual. We hear such individuation in T.S. Eliot, for example, but not in Conrad Aiken. In prose, we speak about

William Faulkner and Ernest Hemingway as stylists—the former whose long, clausal sentences serve emotional complexity, the latter whose relative sparseness evokes emotional austerity.

We tend not to think of, say, Theodore Dreiser and Bernard Malamud as stylists, although surely they have a style. I suspect it's because their subject matter seems to predominate. We read them and say, that's interesting, or become curious about what's going to happen next. We probably can't recognize their sentences or paragraphs as Dreisers or Malamuds, the way we're inclined to say that's a Gerard Manley Hopkins or a Theodore Roethke line, or, for that matter, a Pablo Picasso or Edward Hopper painting.

But I like Dreiser and Malamud. They're page turners. They don't make us stop or pause because of a spectacular phrase. They explore character; their surfaces take us inward with an often welcome transparency. Their rhythms rarely draw attention to themselves. Yet I also very much like to be stopped by moments in a story or poem that at least temporarily are beyond me, or catch me up in their music—to be put in a state of what Donald Justice calls "benign obscurity." I think of Wallace Stevens in this regard, and perhaps all of Hopkins, both of whom I read happily for many years in a state of precognition. As Justice says elsewhere, "Style can slide over into content and nudge it out of the way." I suppose I most prefer style to enhance or help reveal content, but I know what he means.

Style innovates. We see Walt Whitman giving permission to Allen Ginsberg and maybe Robinson Jeffers and Kenneth Rexroth, Galway Kinnell, and recently C.K. Williams. And that other American original Emily Dickinson spawning George Oppen, Denise Levertov, Robert Creeley, E.E. Cummings, to name just a few. W.C. Williams seems like a product of both Whitman and Dickinson—the experiments with punctuation and syntax in her case, and the desire to find and measure an American idiom in his. On their own part are poets like Robert Frost and E.A. Robinson, still influenced by English prosody, but especially in Frost's case adapting it to American cadences and speech.

Yet a straining toward style may be evident when we're unsure that we have anything to say. I know that I resort to dazzle when I'm least confident of my claims. I create a virtual smokescreen of words to conceal an absence of substance. In my interview with Kitchen and Rubin I spoke only positively about style, as if there were no difference between poetry and poeticizing. Style without substance is sad and conspicuous, like a dandy walking into a room where monks have gathered in gray robes to wonder about their souls.

But I'm fond of a few conspicuous stylists who've successfully risked going into new territory. Berryman and his *Dream Songs* comes to mind. As do Marianne Moore and her syllabics.

James Wright's book *The Branch Will Not Break* became, for me and many others of my generation, an important influence. Style could be or appear to be something direct and simple! But, of course, "simple" in Wright's case is an achieved artifice. Prior to that book, and prior to his life falling apart, he wrote traditionally formal poems. We might say he was a rhymer until he realized his life didn't rhyme. No doubt his formal training helped him—the echo of the iamb in almost every line. All the would-be poets I knew in the mid to late sixties wanted to break / Into blossom, or mention places like Martins Ferry or Wheeling, West Virginia, names that stood for a despoiled America.

Which is to say one could be stylish without being fancy. Wright had something interesting to say and a way of saying it that felt necessary. He and the very different Donald Justice and Philip Larkin were among the poets whose work served as beacons back then, and to a large degree still do. Justice was, like Wright, a tonalist, someone who strove to match attitude with event. Unlike Wright, he preferred indirection rather than anything that smacked of "telling it like it is." Unlike Wright, both Justice and Larkin were masters of restraint, with the edge of excellence perhaps going to Larkin whose letters revealed he had more to restrain.

However, the poet I most aspire to be like is Theodore Roethke, whose notion of the personal was more overtly sensual. Late in his life in "The Far Field" and "Meditation at Oyster River" he displayed his meditative gifts with the same fine ear he exhibited in his early poems, though appropriately modulated.

In an essay about style, how can I resist acknowledging someone who'd write, "I caught this morning's minion, king- / dom of daylight's dauphin, dapple-dawn-drawn Falcon" and the countless other lines of brio on the verge of silliness? Nevertheless, I find myself trusting Hopkins's seriousness. He's one of those poets who has rewritten the rules, or proven there aren't any if you're skillful enough. Earlier I said that style innovates, and Hopkins created his own inimitable category. I think it was Eliot who said the most difficult accomplishment for a poet is to introduce a new idiom or rhythm into the language. When such an event occurs, voice and style can blend, become indistinguishable, as I think occurs in the best of Hopkins. And over time, we should only judge writers on their best work.

Probably all writers we admire have developed a voice, a trustworthy way of moving down the page. To have a voice presumes that what is said is also embodied, that what we hear is supported by tone and timbre. But style is not revealed on a single occasion. Style is what is repeated and repeatable. And is merely adornment unless it serves the poem's central concerns. And of this I'm sure: writers who worry about affecting a style will only reveal the effort of seeking one.

Forms and Structures

THE SHORTEST ESSAY I EVER WROTE, maybe the shortest essay anyone has ever written, was called "Little Essay on Form." It went like this: "We build the corral as we reinvent the horse." Later, I added: "Craft is what nails the gate, helps formalize the space, and keeps the horseshit out of the picture. It leaves us with the necessary."

I was rather pleased with my epigrammatic self, yet I knew that if I were to continue in that reductive mode I might be on my way to a kind of incredulity. Metaphor pushed too far will always be on the verge of collapsing. That's why the exquisite metaphor or simile pleases us so. It goes to the precipice, dangles, and survives. In it resides a recklessness, a groping in thin air toward an unknown correlative. Eliot has Prufrock say, ". . . the evening is spread out against the sky." How so? Well, "Like a patient etherised upon a table." You can't get much more successfully reckless than that, but I take that back. Maybe architect Frank Gehry has gone further in some of his finest creations.

The imagination plays a large role in the creation of structures or forms, even in relatively fixed forms like the sonnet. Either we're working within chosen confines, our details pressing up against boundaries and those boundaries pressing back, or we're seeking other kinds of restraints that will hold in place our wanderings. Or both. Each approach presents its own demands and opportunities.

I want to look at a poem of mine that wandered toward what I think are its necessities. Some years ago, I was lucky enough to be at the MacDowell Colony with Catherine Ingraham, an architect, who was clearly the most interesting person there. One day she told me a story about Peter Eisenman, who had designed Ohio State University's Wexner Center, in which there is a column that hangs down mid-air and does not connect with the ground. At artist colonies, at least for me, snippets of conversation heard at meals get appropriated, and stories get happily stolen and/or transformed. And that's exactly what happened. I went back to my studio and wrote "The Stairway," which is based on Catherine's story but creates different terms. It's written in free verse, which for me means it's a poem that was seeking its formal properties as it was composed.

The Stairway

The architect wanted to build a stairway
and suspend it with silver, almost invisible
guy wires in a high-ceilinged room,
a stairway you couldn't ascend or descend
except in your dreams. But first—
because wild things are not easily seen
if what's around them is wild—
he'd make sure the house that housed it
was practical, built two-by-four by
two-by-four, slat by slat, without ornament.
The stairway would be an invitation
to anyone who felt invited by it,
and depending on your reaction he'd know
if friendship were possible.
The house he'd claim as his, but the stairway
would be designed to be ownerless,
tilted against any suggestion of a theology,
disappointing to those looking for politics.
Of course the architect knew
that over the years he'd have to build
other things the way others desired,
knew that to live in this world was to trade
a few industrious hours for one beautiful one.
Yet every night when he got home
he could imagine, as he walked in the door,
his stairway going nowhere, not for sale,
and maybe some you to whom nothing
about it need be explained, waiting,
the wine decanted, the night about to unfold.

In mediating what Catherine told me about the architect, I became aware, perhaps by mid-poem, that I was writing an ars poetica. That is, I knew that the architect's creation was suggestive of working habits and perhaps a sensibility that were analogous to mine. The architect builds a stairway that is beautifully useless. In so doing, he has removed himself from the world of art as commodity; his creation is its own reward. In the telling, I was as concerned about the selection and phrasing of details, their tone and the pacing of them, as I was about the story itself—which I was reinventing as well as reconstructing. The architect's stairway is ownerless, one of those creations so magical he can't claim it as belonging wholly to himself. The house that houses it, however, is solid and practical: it draws little attention to itself (not unlike my poem's block form); it is a vehicle for the suspended stairway, nothing more. I let the architect dream of one person who would perfectly understand what he had made, to whom no explanations were necessary, though I don't remember making a decision in that regard. I suppose by this time Catherine's story about the architect was sufficiently my story: I felt no allegiance to what she had told me; I could extend things as I so felt. Ah, to be understood—the refuge and solace of the artist, especially one who can't make a living from his work.

I don't wish to romanticize either poets or architects. The architect, more often than not, is designing buildings in tandem with others and is in the habit of working out effective compromises. He understands "that to live in this world [is] to trade / a few industrious hours for one beautiful one." Poets generally have more freedom to be wild, reckless, but if they are good poets they want that wildness harnessed because they are simultaneously seeking limits. Shortly after the first hot rush of composition, they will have brought to their work the cold eye of the problem solver. It's trench work after that.

Robert Frost's "Stopping by Woods on a Snowy Evening" is a poem—with its iambic tetrameter and rhymed quatrains—that has more conspicuous formalities than mine. His solution to the rhyme pattern in his famous last stanza is one of the poem's brilliant moves, a move made possible because of the poem's established regularities. Here's what Frost says about the poem's genesis and development, as reported in Reginald Cook's

The Dimensions of Robert Frost. (If Frost's statement had had a title, it might have been "Structure as a series of commitments.")

> "I can have my first line any way I please," Frost says, "but once I say a line I am committed. The first line IS a commitment . . ." He goes on to say how he could have written the next line so that he'd be working in couplets, and worried then that he'd have to have couplets all the way. But no, he says, he was dancing, he was free. Then he found himself writing, 'He will not see me stopping here,' the poem's third line, and felt uncommitted, or perhaps he'd written a line that he knew would be seeking but had not yet found what it might be committed to. "For the three rhymes in the next stanza," he says, "I picked up the unrhymed line in the first stanza" ('He will not see me stopping here'), which began for him a way of interlocking his stanzas. "Every step you take is a further commitment," Frost concludes, and disarmingly admits, "For my poem is a commitment to convention." He then offers what we've come to understand as a characteristic Frostian counter-thought: "The interest is [in?] the quarrel with those commitments."

Frost had established a pattern he could break away from, and the timing of the break serves to accentuate the poem's emotional import. In essence, the structural unfolding of the poem becomes a link to its content—the commitment to "promises," to leaving, to staying awake. His poem is an example of how strict form can facilitate ingenuity and a deepening of concerns.

Compositional sloppiness, on the other hand, delimits possibility. W.D. Snodgrass sought to demonstrate this in a sequence called *De/Compositions*. He wanted to have some instructive fun with well-known poems such as Frost's by tampering with their diction and metrics, and he did. Here's Frost's poem, and then Snodgrass's. Let's call Frost's the carefully made house. The other, as you will see, will fail inspection.

Stopping by Woods on a Snowy Evening

Whose woods these are I think I know.
His house is in the village, though;
He will not see me stopping here
To watch his woods fill up with snow.

My little horse must think it queer
To stop without a farmhouse near
Between the woods and frozen lake
The darkest evening of the year.

He gives his harness bells a shake
To ask if there is some mistake.
The only other sound's the sweep
Of easy wind and downy flake.

The woods are lovely, dark and deep,
But I have promises to keep,
And miles to go before I sleep,
And miles to go before I sleep.

Passing by Woods During a Snowfall
        —de/composed from Frost

Who owns these woodlands I don't know
But they live somewhere else and so
They won't mind that I've come out here
To see the lovely falling snow.

My horse must wonder why we're here
On back roads though no one lives here
Next to a forest and a lake
Where it's so cold this time of year.

He gives his windblown mane a shake
To ask which way he ought to take
But I'm enchanted by the sweep
Of wind and whispers of snowflake.

The woods lie clad in beauty deep
But Man has schedules he must keep.
I've got to go home now and sleep;
I've got to go home now and sleep.

I don't want to spend a lot of time on what I trust is obvious, but from the clunky first line that begins the de/composition all the way to the abominable last quatrain we feel—I'll put it nicely—in the presence of a writer who exhibits throughout that he values content more than the handling of content. Let me also put it less nicely. As the poet's tin ear suggests, Snodgrass is imitating someone who probably hasn't read very much or very well. Nothing in his history of reading or writing would make him wince when he wrote, "The woods lie clad in beauty deep / But Man has schedules he must keep."

Snodgrass's burlesquing of Frost's poem is deliberately broad, but it makes us think how the smallest of alterations might ruin a good line, e.g., "And ten miles to go before I sleep, / And ten miles to go before I sleep." Not only would "ten" provide an extra syllable, and thus break the iambic flow, but we'd be left thinking about specific distance rather than the "miles" that could represent a lifetime.

The best practitioners take great care with the smallest of things; the worst seem to think that there's an intrinsic value to what they've found themselves doing and saying. The carpenter who poorly frames a door doesn't go around saying how well it shuts. Sloppiness embarrasses him. But I've heard many would-be poets defending the equivalent of a poorly made door. They actually believe that how they feel about something is important. Beginning poets—and for all I know, beginning architects—take note: conscientious artisans never believe that how they feel is more important than how they execute.

I'd like to wander back for a moment to the corral. The corral is easy to see as a fixed structure, but the implication of my one-line essay is that the corral doesn't fully become what it is until the experience that occurs within it is made vital by transformation. Different degrees of ambition, of course, create different challenges. So I can imagine that even an empty corral could be made interesting, for instance by someone who saw it as a structure within a structure, someone whose aim was to explore a vision of an entire ranch and its interrelationships. The artist would have more space to formalize, more horseshit to hide. The fun might be just beginning.

"The maximum amount of wildness the form can bear," is what Donald Justice wanted from an ideal poem. If you didn't know his aesthetics, you might think he had "Howl" in mind, but more likely he was thinking of poems by Emily Dickinson or Weldon Kees. Nevertheless, "Howl" seems to qualify nicely as an example of Justice's statement. Wouldn't the New York and Bilbao Guggenheims also qualify? As I said earlier, form is the pressure the artist puts on material in order to see what it can bear. Form's primary aim is paradoxical: to exclude and accommodate. It wants to make room, for example, for odd shapes and strange companions. Essentially, form's job is to help reveal content. It's in the business of heightening, subordinating, arranging. It controls rates of disclosure, degrees of importance. Form guides the eye.

Or maybe form's job is to be a thing unto itself.

Frank Lloyd Wright said, "The small house is the architect's greatest challenge." I suspect that poets who have experimented with heroic couplets or the haiku would know what he meant. With compression, any error is magnified. As with Snodgrass's de/composition or a failed bungalow, there's this terribly conspicuous thing in front of you. Wright seems at his best when he could bring his imagination not just to the design of a particular house but to how it would fit into a neighborhood, and become both a part of and an extension of its environment. I'm thinking in particular of his Fallingwater, which happens to stand just fifty miles from where I live.

The small house may be the architect's greatest challenge, but the large, ambitious structure should be handled by the architect or poet as if it presented equally difficult problems. Of course, the viewer only wants something splendid to admire and think about. Anyone who has looked hard at Notre Dame or the Taj Mahal, or tried to get a sure handle on *Paradise Lost* or *The Waste Land*, knows the opportunities for exploration in structures to which form has given the feel of permanence. The larger the structure the more numerous the opportunities. And depending on where you're standing in relation to them—physically, psychologically, historically—such structures take on different properties. Coherence is an invitation into their mysteries, permitting rather than restricting speculation. That which is sloppily constructed, on the other hand, permits more viewpoints than are useful.

A master of forms, that very scrupulous and mischievous "sculptor" Andy Goldsworthy contends that "all forms are to be found in nature" and adds, "By exploring them, I hope to understand the whole. My work needs to include the loose and disordered as well as the tight and regular." He believes that he's "in collaboration with nature," which is a necessary fiction for him. What he actually does is impose on nature what is inherent, so that what we're looking at is a semblance of what is already there. More than anything else, what we're looking at is a Goldsworthy.

Looking at almost any Goldsworthy construction, I'm reminded of these lines from Wallace Stevens's "Anecdote of a Jar."

> I placed a jar in Tennessee,
> And round it was, upon a hill.
> It made the slovenly wilderness
> Surround that hill.
>
> The wilderness rose up to it,
> And sprawled around, no longer wild.

Art gives us a vantage point, a way of seeing. The jar formalizes the wilderness just as the man-made corral might focus an observer's eye and make the whole ranch less amorphous.

In many ways, Goldsworthy's work reminds us that art is not like what we recognize as experience, but rather is a fully realized arrangement of gestures and moves, an imitation of experience, an enactment that moments before did not exist. The sculpture intensifies something previously half known or half seen and is an object in its own right.

Though Goldsworthy's work tilts toward underlying patterns in the natural world, it also borrows its symmetries and discordancies from the history of art and architecture. We see the pyramids he makes out of rocks, in any of his various arches, in the surreality of his ice sculptures. He surprisingly transforms the known, then further defamiliarizes it by doing something else to it—in one instance by placing a dead heron's feathers and cut stone in among stacked branches, in another by building a giant, moonlike snowball into the bare branches of a tree. Pure mischief. Beauty happens by means of the permission he gives himself to construct it: the result is the vitalization of landscape.

I've mostly been talking about form as if achieving it were more or less rational. Isn't there always something secretly propulsive about how the best art gets made? Let's call it "the unknown agent x," which is what Nabokov called the most influential force that molds a human being. Heredity and environment, he says, take second and third place to it. This unknown agent x has formal or structural implications as well.

"Prudent Triangle," written by the Yugoslav poet Vasko Popa and translated by Charles Simic, might be a paradigm for what mysteriously drives a poem:

Prudent Triangle

Once upon a time there was a triangle
It had three sides
The fourth it kept hidden
In its burning center

By day it climbed its three peaks
And admired its center
At night it rested
In one of its three angles

Each dawn it watched its three sides
Turn into three fiery wheels
And vanish in the blue of never return

It took its fourth side
Embraced and broke it three times
To hide it again in its old place

And again it had only three sides
And again it climbed each day
To its three peaks

And admired its center
While at night it rested
in one of its three angles

Perhaps the triangle is prudent because—although it has a fourth side, an agent x, a side that is active all day—at night it rested / in one of its angles." The triangle knows when not to be active, knows when it's better off "admiring its burning center." At some point, therefore, it has distance, aesthetic distance, which of course is analogous to Popa's participation in his own poem. Surely, "Prudent Triangle" invites other readings, but for my purposes the way the triangle behaves is emblematic of structural fluidity.

The fourth side is the agent of heat, a propulsive force altering our conventional understanding of the triangle. By day, the triangle's three sides "turn into three fiery wheels / and vanish in the blue of never return." The triangle just "watches" this happen, implying that what it has set in motion has imperatives of its own. Then the triangle takes its fourth side and breaks it "three times / to hide it again in its old place." Here the triangle is active and full of intention. I take this as a metaphor for the poem's energy, the energy that is a combination of the poet's intentionality and the poem's vibrant, increasingly insistent demands.

The triangle—and by extension the poet—is an orchestrator of its mysteries, sometimes admiring its elements from afar, or watching as its parts seem to act by themselves, or very close and involved, embracing and breaking. As with my corral metaphor, I would be wrong to push Popa's little "once upon a time" fairy tale too far, but a discussion about a poem's form is often incomplete unless it identifies the poem's main structural propulsive forces, which are likely linked to its central concerns.

The more able the artist, the more he or she can accommodate the unruly, the serendipitous, the discordant—in a sense manage the unmanageable—and to create for these disparate energies a livable environment. To do this, the artist must know something about commitments, small and large. Though form seems to represent restriction, forms in art offer opportunities. We need an expansive Walt Whitman for every idiosyncratic Emily Dickinson, a Louis Kahn for every Philip Johnson. But when we're speaking of form we need to remember at least two different kinds of excellence. One is represented by the stairway whose stairs no one will ever use and by Goldsworthy's often evanescent structures. The other is represented by all those poems and buildings that attempt to frame and house what's human. I want my structures to be habitable, with doors opening into spaces that intrigue. I want to cast a light on what is there but not easily seen. For a poet to forget that one of his jobs is to explore what it feels like to be alive in a particular place and time is the equivalent of an architect forgetting that houses are meant to be lived in.

Refuge, and the Serious Humor of Kafka and Beckett

THE WRITER HOLED UP IN A GARRET, or in search of a room of her own—those are the images of an artist's workplace that most of us aspiring artists grew up with. There was, of course, a romance associated with them. They weren't safe places as much as they were refuges, places of retreat and struggle where the writer attempted to eke out an existence while courting the muse, or, more accurately the world.

Later, with a little good fortune, perhaps the garret becomes the studio. And the room, well, maybe you learn to close the door to it.

A few weeks after I was asked to write about such concerns, and declined, I moved into the realm of what might be called second thought/better thought. The subject began to engage me. I'd resist the stereotypical writer-in-the-garret sense of refuge and travail; instead I'd write about the refuge of cowardice, or of charm, or of small ambition. I thought about the various ways I'd hidden in my life, and those times I'd not risked going as far or as deep as I might have.

Then a lucky thing happened, if luck for a writer is an occasion to regard something differently. I found myself once again teaching Kafka's "A Hunger Artist," that wry parable about an artist who takes his art to the limit. Or is it Kafka's elaborate pun about the starving artist? Whichever, it's teacherly fun to talk about a concept like professional fasting going out of fashion, no longer a spectator sport, and the protagonist suddenly able to pursue his art on his own terms—the circus, his new employer, imposing no constraints. We see him getting thinner and thinner in his cage while the public walks by, uninterested.

My favorite moment is when he has almost reached the limit of his "artistry," and is asked by the overseer, "Are you still fasting? When on earth do you mean to stop?" Kafka could have had the hunger artist say something noble as his last words, but instead, after telling the overseer that he shouldn't admire his fasting, and after being asked why, the hunger artist says, "Because I have to fast, I can't help it." And then adds, "Because I couldn't find the food I liked. If I had found it, believe me, I should have made no fuss and stuffed myself like you or anyone else." After his death, he's replaced in the cage by a young, vital panther.

So, by temperament and taste, this artist, who apparently does not live in any other world, neither social nor political, acts as if his only choice is to be an Artist. In the freedom of his cage he's safe to pursue his art because it's his calling and nobody cares. There's an obvious bitterness here, which Kafka's sad professional life accounts for, but there's a humor present too, which his life doesn't account for, and which is his vision and his genius. I became aware, more than ever, that austerity would never be my ticket to the palace of art. And I was never sure that excess would be my ticket either. The story had never seemed so personal—so confrontational, really.

The driven artist, like anyone who might go all the way with some endeavor, pays a social cost. With great artists, history has a way of privileging their behaviors. Greatness has its rewards. The rest of us toil in a more pay-for-your-actions world. If we take refuge in our rooms for days on end, it's best that we live alone. If we live with others, we'd better emerge with something pretty good. Magnificent would be preferable. And even if we do emerge with something of consequence, there's no guarantee it will offset, say, feelings of spousal neglect. The alternative is to live with a saint, about which there are many downsides, not the least of which is that in most saints lurks a revolutionary; it's just a matter of time before the upheavals begin.

My truth is that I also live in worlds that splinter off from the artistic, and have sought refuge in sports, sex, the classroom, to name just a few. Therefore, I know something about the way such retreats can satisfy, but also how satisfaction can conceal yourself from yourself, and how complacency is always nearby, feet up on the ottoman as you conjure a sentence that only the unread might think profound. There are no safe havens—for long.

And there are refuges that are just watering holes on the way to nowhere. The refuge of the habitual—the comfort of it, the stasis. The refuge of wishing to please—those little forays into hackdom that injure the soul. The refuge of the lie, how it buys time, lets you ride for a while in its big white car.

I tell my students the public wants the sleek young panther, wants it in its cage, wants excitement without danger, wants the artist to be considerate enough to stop before his bones show, to please not be so tacky as to disturb. I talk about the refuge of the neatly wrapped package. The refuge of the melodious. But only lately have I told them that the hunger artist scares me.

The virtues of refuge need not be argued. From the Underground Railroad to those who hide the Anne Franks of the world, from the needs of the displaced to the great decency of those who provide shelter and food, the word refuge has earned its good name. My personal examples of such refuge, as I said earlier, are small by comparison. The friend who gave me her house rent-free after I became a refugee of my marriage. The many residencies I've had at the artist colonies, Yaddo and MacDowell. The homes I've lived in as child and adult that have been places of normal retreat—places, as Robert Frost reminds me, I haven't had to deserve.

Books have been my most enduring refuge, not the ones I've written, but the ones I've read—my good, long disappearances into them—and how they always return me to a newly recognizable, enlarged world with more places to hide, get lost, be found. A great book is a refuge as well as an encyclopedia for the negatively capable, those of us more or less at home with uncertainties, not yet made entirely miserable by the burden of consciousness. But I've also found comrades in books merely good, even mediocre. I've loved how some authors manage to give, if not refuge, then a kind of temporary home to the displaced, the misunderstood, the estranged. Kafka makes me feel sane. He dramatized aspects of my unarticulated life. No refuge for him, though. He had no schoolyard to escape to when things went bad, as I did. When Barbara Winokur broke up with me when I was sixteen, I dropped the phone and left the house and played ferocious, cathartic basketball until dark. Also Kafka had no father who told him that he was the best third baseman he'd ever seen. Can I call such events lucky? Would the answer confuse life with art?

The hunger artist had only his art, and when faced with rejection and neglect he had no place to go except further inward, that dangerous province where only the touchy-feely find solace. Get in touch with your feelings, they say, as if all feelings were sanguine and sweet. Kafka would have laughed. He'd have his hunger artist shed another pound. He sent his hunger artist inward where success was concomitant with annihilation. That's scary enough. What's the thin line between artistic courage and artistic suicide?

To the extent that Kafka was his hunger artist, his parable probably scared him as well, but Kafka, in a most important way, wasn't the hunger artist. He was the hunger artist's maker, and was amused by what he made. Unlike the hunger artist, Kafka was able to look outward as well as inward, and he understood that the enemies of true seriousness are often compositional sobriety and earnestness. It's the handling of subject matter—Kafka's inventiveness and élan and management of detail—that challenges me the most. How to avoid the torpidity of the somber when your subject is somber? Well, maybe it helps if you believe, as Kafka did, that life is an awful joke. Maybe world-view can propel even the most socialized artist beyond his self-consciousness. In the classroom, as I spoke, I knew I was talking to myself.

Samuel Beckett, another literary hero of mine, in his work invented a dark playground, gave his characters ingenious monkey bars on which to cavort, swings that promised a return of sorts, but to a world without solace. They played and they waited, and when they weren't worried they were either foolish or afraid. Meanwhile, his work would give unhappiness a lilt and a song. Kafka was more situationally comic. We need only to think of Gregor turning into a bug in "The Metamorphosis," and the seriocomic circumstances that follow. Then we remember certain "bug" jobs we've had, and/or certain families we've observed or been part of, and the absurd becomes an exaggeration of the real, or should I say becomes like some awful disfigurement, suddenly identifiable once a societal mask has been lifted. Beckett's Vladimir and Estragon were designed to amuse us while they amuse themselves, until every silence reminds them they—and by extension we—are terribly alone, and no one's coming to remedy the fear and alienation. Their plight is situational, too, but the situation feels more inescapably metaphysical.

Are we pleased, if not made happy, by the human condition so artfully delivered? I am. Is there refuge in being put in agreement with reality? For me, yes, a strange, mostly yes. Often, like most people. I'm content to live in the world of illusion, a kind of refuge in itself. There may be only small comfort in knowing that if there's any salvation to be had that it's not going to come from above, but in well-rendered versions of our predicaments. After all, when others would be depressed by Ingmar Bergman movies, I would find myself elated by how well despair and angst had been depicted.

I don't mean to compare myself with either Beckett or Kafka. My subject is refuge, not talent or success. The majority of my writing life has been in the shadows. I suppose there are advantages to that; if few care about what you're doing you can almost do anything you want. Yet I never desired the refuge of being unrecognized. Even when I've gotten some attention, there was—beneath a veneer of accomplishment—an interior life that was full of emptiness and longing. Great writers, like Beckett and Kafka, deliver that world to us. From a certain distance, a writer's neediness is as hilarious as it is genuine.

I came of age as a writer, certainly as a poet, when the romance of self-destruction was omnipresent. Booze, drugs, suicide, the virtues of suffering, were emblems of the enterprise, if not by open advocacy, then by example. John Berryman, Randell Jarrell, Delmore Schwartz, Sylvia Plath, Weldon Kees, Anne Sexton—well, it seemed to me that there was an enormous and necessary price to pay if you wanted to be good. Theodore Roethke and James Wright, two of my favorites, died in their early fifties— could I be a significant poet and escape such a fate? I must admit that I gave certain aspects of self-destruction their fair chance. But I came to realize that to seek suffering was stupid. It would come to you in time; you didn't have to seek it.

I remember taking to heart Flaubert's advice. "Be regular and orderly in your daily life, so you can be wild and original in your work." And sometime later, from Jean Valentine's essay on Plath, putting this in my notebook: "In my experience and deepest belief, poetry is a lifeline, not a deathline; the poet, if she dies, dies in spite of her poetry, not because of it."

There's no telling how far life's circumstances will make us go, or just how many things are out there, sure to confound our plans. Maybe, too, artistic bravery is always something of an accident, some combination of discovery and formal attentiveness. So much is beyond our control. And there's no telling in advance how, by solving, for instance, a problem of tone or pacing, we find ourselves saying something radically true. There is refuge in process. As Kafka wrote at the end of another of his parables, this one about the Sirens, "It would be doing them an injustice to say they wanted to seduce; they knew they had claws and sterile wombs, and they lamented this aloud. They could not help it that their laments sounded so beautiful."

2

Locker Room Talk

HAVING BEEN ATHLETIC MOST OF MY LIFE, I've spent a fair amount of time in locker rooms and have overheard my share of "locker room talk." For reasons I couldn't understand for many years, I rarely participated in it and certainly never felt smug or superior about my lack of participation. In fact, I felt quite the opposite; I thought something was wrong with me. As a teenager and well into my twenties, I'd hear someone recount his latest real or wishful conquest, there'd be a kind of general congratulatory laughter, tacit envy, but what I remember feeling most was wonderment and then embarrassment.

There was, of course, little or no public information about sex when I was growing up in the forties and fifties. The first time I heard someone talk about having sex was in the school yard (the locker room without walls) when I was twelve or thirteen. Frankie Salvo, a big boy of sixteen, made it sound dirty, something great you do with a bad girl. It was my first real experience with pornography and it was thrilling; a little terrifying, too. My mind conjured its pictures. Wonderment. Not wonderful.

Some years later, after experience, wonderment gave way to embarrassment. I wasn't sure for whom I was embarrassed, the girl spoken about, the storyteller, or myself. Nevertheless, I understood the need to tell. I, too, wanted to tell my good friend, Alan, but for some reason I never told him very much. In retrospect, it was my first test with what Robert Frost calls knowing "the delicacy of when to stop short," a delicacy I took no pride in. I felt excessively private, cut off.

I began thinking about all of this recently because in the locker room at college a young man was telling his friend—loud enough for all of us to hear—what he did to this particular young woman the night before and what she did to him. It was clear how important it was for him to impress his friend, far more important than the intimacy itself, as if the sexual act weren't complete until he had completed it among other men.

This time I knew something about the nature of my embarrassment. It wasn't just that he had cheapened himself in the telling, but, like all things that embarrass us, it had struck some part of me that was complicitous, to a degree guilty, the kind of guilt you feel every time there's a discrepancy between what you know you're supposed to feel (correct feelings) and what in fact you've thought of, if not done. But more than that, I was embarrassed by the young man's assumption—culturally correct for the most part—that we other men in the locker room were his natural audience. There were five or six of us, and we certainly didn't boo or hiss. Those of us who were silent (all of us except his friend) had given our quiet sanctions.

What did it all mean? That men, more often than not, in a very fundamental way prefer other men? Or was it all about power, an old story, success with women as a kind of badge, an accoutrement of power? Was the young man saying to the rest of us, "I'm powerful"? I thought so for a while, but then I thought that he seemed to be saying something different. He was saying out loud to himself and to the rest of us that he hadn't succumbed to the greatest loss of power, yielding to the attractiveness and power of women, which could mean admitting he felt something or, at the furthest extreme, had fallen in love.

From Samson, to the knight in Keats's poem "La Belle Dame Sans Merci," to countless examples in world literature, the warning is clear: women take away your power. To fall in love with one is to be distracted from the world of accomplishment and acquisitiveness. But to have sex and then to talk about it publicly is a kind of final protection, the ultimate pro-phylactic against the dangers of feeling.

"Love means always having to say you're sorry," a friend once said to me. That had its truth, and it implied—among other things—a mature love, a presumption of mutual respect and equality. On some level, the young man in the locker room sensed and feared such a relationship. He had ventured into the dark and strange world of women and had come out unscathed, literally untouched. He was back with us, in the locker room, which was the country he understood and lived in, with immunity. He thought we'd be happy for him.

God, Democracy, Trump, James Hollis, and the American People

Time for H.L. Mencken Again

SEVERAL YEARS AGO, LISTENING TO THE DEBATE on healthcare reform, I was struck by how each side was sure it knew what The American People wanted, and felt no particular necessity to offer evidence for their certainties. Many of the same political soothsayers also have pipelines to God. They know what He's thinking, too. They begin sentences with constructions like "God willing" when they mean "If we can." No one calls them on it. Even the more liberal-minded are not above such shamelessness. Granted, when it comes to what is or isn't knowable, there's more evidence that The American People actually exist than that God does, but who are The American People, really? They're definitely not a single entity. I'm one of them, and so is the banker and the cabbie, not to mention my neighbor who beats his wife.

A vote along party lines in our name is a kind of fundamentalism—ideology trumping the difficulty of careful discernment. Another name for it, I suppose, is politics.

Though Obama risked displaying intelligence and eloquence in a country that remains suspicious of those qualities, he too spoke about The American People with a broad authority that is, at best, sentimental. Where is H.L. Mencken when we need him? Where is someone who would at least think it paradoxical that democracy tends to work, while daring to point out how many of The American People are ruled by superstition and other forms of ignorance? The American People elected George W. Bush. Now we have Donald Trump, someone who doesn't read, is crass and dishonest, and nevertheless appeals to a segment of the population that apparently can overlook such defects, which seem to become more blatantly conspicuous every day.

In 1996, I wrote, "It is appalling that some people—the mendacious, the uninformed—can vote. Yet worse if they could not. Oddly, the majority does have an intelligence, sleepy-keen, animal-like, most brilliant when injured or wronged." Now I'd substitute "dangerous" for "brilliant." But I do know that people worldwide seek the freedoms and rights that many of us take for granted. Democracy has its flaws, and, strictly speaking, may be more accurately described as an oligarchy. But whatever our system is, changes in power have mostly occurred without anything like a palace coup.

"The people have spoken, the bastards," Huey Long said after losing an election. He did not try to mobilize those bastards into revolt. Democracy has always insured that every few years the bad guys and the good guys get shuffled, redefined. This may happen again in two years. But I can't help but feel an urgency for some large revolt to occur. I'd be happy with impeachment, which would leave us, I know, not with peace but with Pence, who believes God is on our side, and also in policies that will set us back into an intellectual stone age. Trump, too, may believe God is on his side, and probably would claim an intimacy with Him. *Such a good God, a friend really, the best deity there is, believe me,* we can hear him say.

"Quarrels with others produce rhetoric," W.B. Yeats said, "quarrels with oneself produce poetry." Yes, I say. Nevertheless I want to quarrel with certain American people, especially those who would support their Trumpian arguments with Trumpian-talk. Fake this and fake that, adjectives like "crooked" and "loser" and other diminishments that finally apply more to him than to his adversaries. Mencken would have eaten Trump for breakfast. I'd like a part of him with every meal. Yeats's statement has informed my work for years, yet I want to also believe that quarrels with others, without any complicity, can satisfy, depending on the subject. The Holocaust, for example. I'm thinking of Paul Celan's "Death Fugue" and say William Styron's *Sophie's Choice,* dramatizations of an evil so pure that Trump's behavior merely seems vulgar and mean-spirited by comparison. Perhaps in this regard we can only say that Trump has never had a quarrel with himself.

Here's Mencken from his *Treatise on the Gods*: "The great majority of men and women. . . probably do not know precisely what they believe, but the general cast of their thought is still toward something passing under the name of faith." Mencken wrote this in 1930. Doesn't it still seem accurate? "Men otherwise highly enlightened," he goes on to say, "cling maudlinly to ideas that go back to the infancy of the human race. Worse, they assume that what they thereby permit themselves to believe, irrationally and against all the known facts, is a kind of knowledge."

Many people believe they are being honest when they say what they think. "To thine own self be true" may be good advice for the introspective, but rather disastrous to those who live unexamined lives. The unreliable narrator never knows how others hear him. "The American People . . . ," he says, and someone in the back row is giggling. If I were giving a speech and Mencken were in the audience, I'd be worried. He was a deconstructionist long before anyone heard of Derrida.

God bless America, for example, on the face of it, is a harmless enough sentiment, a short nationalistic prayer that has, in parlance, taken on the currency of a slogan. I imagine it most troubles theologians who might worry what kind of self-respecting God could be moved to such favoritism. But Mencken, I think, would see in it either disingenuousness or a great historical innocence.

He would know that some senators and members of Congress actually believe that God is on their side, and that some others merely find the saying of it politically efficacious. Either way, the country—aka The American People—does not break into laughter or protest when such things are declared, though many of us feel as the alienated Trump supporters must feel. We listen incredulously to descriptions of us, not recognizing a thing we are said to think.

At least, however, we can recognize what we don't think. Trump seems to have no core of belief or non-belief, and he discovers his attitudes (too ill-formed to be called "positions") as he tweets or speaks them. He contradicts himself, not because he contains multitudes, but because he contains vacuities. This, too, Mencken foresaw: leaders who reflect back to the people their own empty souls. He warned of this type in 1920. "As democracy is perfected," he wrote, "the office [of the Presidency] represents, more and more closely, the inner soul of the people . . . On some great and glorious day, the plain folks of the land will reach their heart's desire at last, and the White House will be adorned by a downright fool and a complete narcissistic moron." Mencken's famous contempt for the average American, the class of people he called the "booboisie," sometimes undermined his persuasiveness. I love his sentence that contains "the inner soul of the people." In the one that follows, I sense his wit yielding to its inferior form of mockery, sarcasm.

"Existence is an intolerable riddle," Mencken notes in one of his few gestures of sympathy to why people turn to religion for solace. He knows that it takes strength to live without answers, amid uncertainties. How to live in the dark? What if the riddle is unsolvable? The best thinking from the best religions can guide us part way. All the better if it's combined with the best that's ever been thought or said from, say, Aristotle to Kant to Rawls. But Mencken remains wary of the priest as well as the politician, by which he means the interpreter of dogma or policy, whom he says "is always willing to sacrifice every other sort of good to the one good of his Arcanum—the vague body of mysteries that he calls the truth."

We should begin to worry when power shifts to people with allegiance to only one book, or one-party line, or to a Donald Trump, who we might wish had more Machiavelli in him. Machiavelli made hypocrisy an art form. He knew that a ruler must give the illusion of transparency while making secret agreements and forging back-room deals. In *The Prince* he argues that all effective leaders should be, to some degree, nationalists, but back-room nationalists who serve themselves and their countries with what becomes useful chicanery. Trump, on the other hand, isn't clever enough to sugarcoat his deceptions. His lies are conspicuous. He says what he means, but is tone-deaf to the resonance of his proclamations. And he most dangerously is a nationalist in a world whose concerns must be global. He needs a more sophisticated hypocrisy if he hopes to succeed, perhaps one that gives the illusion of global cooperation.

This age could also profit by the wisdom of Jungian psychoanalyst James Hollis, perhaps the smartest man I personally know. In an essay on Narcissus he offers, among other insights, "The pitiful truth of narcissism is that *the narcissist stares in the mirror and no one stares back.*" What Trump sees when he stares in the mirror is an image he believes to be himself. He admires what he sees; the nothing that stares back flatters him. Only when he speaks does he become visible; to others, that is. That is why the narcissist doesn't apologize and has no regrets. Hollis, citing Jung, says "what is denied inwardly, will come to us as fate."

Those American people who support Trump are not deplorable, but don't believe what Heraclitus stated and every self-respecting novelist knows: character is destiny. Trump's "base" values action or promises of action over character. Even if now and then they get what they want, they don't see that the results are tainted by the company they keep and the people they admire. The "good people" who hang around with anti-Semites and chant Nazi slogans might at other times of the day be kind to their wives. Some may have mastered the art of the deal, and learned a few dirty tricks about getting ahead. History will reveal who they are. It may be frustrating to many of us that their "fate" has not yet occurred.

Mencken thought that the Bible was great poetry, which it is. It says nothing specific, of course, about The American People, but is often very evocative about people, their foibles and their virtues. Good literature, which Trump shows little knowledge of, works that way. You can take it with you to other countries. It resonates. It complicates. "Equipment for living," Kenneth Burke called it. The full truth of a matter is always somewhat elusive. Those who want immediate results are usually not truth's pursuants. But every age needs an iconoclast like Mencken to keep an eye on what needs to be corrected, to help put us in some agreement with the real, with what, in fact, goes on.

I once claimed that in order to register a successful complaint one has to demonstrate at least a degree of complicity. I hereby take back some of what I said. We're many months now into Trump's presidency, and I can't think of a week that has gone by in which he hasn't said something stupid and/or cruel. Here's Hollis again, this time I think to complicate matters: "Hysterical rhetoric is precisely the uncertainty of authority as it defends itself against its own anxiety." It's a statement that could apply to me as well as to Trump and his followers. I don't think my claims are hysterical, though I wish them to be as provocative as Mencken's are. And I admit that when it comes to Trump I'm full of anxiety. No doubt Trumpians would sense my anxiety, and deem my claims as unfair and prejudiced. Moreover, as Peter Wehner recently wondered in a New York Times op-ed piece, "Am I missing something good about Trump?" He admits that it's impossible for him to see Trump from a distance, dispassionately, that his (Wehner's) views, even if basically accurate, are also "incomplete and probably distorted."

Is it too easy to feel superior to a Trump? Perhaps. To his base? Well, not as easy. I think of his "base" as I thought of some of my students who were enrolled in my Literature and Ethics class. I'd pose the following question to the entire class at our first meeting. Would you kill, by pressing a button, a non-descript peasant in a foreign land with the guarantee of never getting caught, for which you would receive a million dollars? They could answer anonymously, but had to give a reason or reasons. There were twenty-five people in class. Two out of twenty-five would press the button in 1992. By 1997 the figure rose incrementally to eleven. Reasons: It would just be a one-time thing. Or, why not, it's a dog-eat-dog world. (One student wrote "a doggy-dog world.) Afterward, I would tell them the question was asked only to see how many of them were murderers. There'd always be a few gasps. I'd like to think by the end of each semester I had made a few of the murderers rethink their position.

My guess is that Trump's base is mostly made up of people who in various ways feel deprived or screwed-over, who have legitimate gripes, yet are not repulsed by characterless people like Trump, with a history of exploitation of people like themselves. The button pushers (those with an undeveloped moral conscience) constitute just part of his supporters. The rest justify their positions with passages from the Bible or hand-me-down truths from their parents, or with a profound sense of being neglected. I can think of circumstances in which I might be one of them.

Let's go steal a car, a friend once said to me. He thought it would be fun. I said no. I didn't have to think about it; I didn't steal cars. That decision did not ipso facto make me a moral person. I had absorbed Aristotle's wisdom that to call yourself a good person was never a one-time act. I didn't have to think about my friend's proposition because to not steal had become something habitual, long thought about and resolved. Yet if my child were injured and I had no other way of getting to a hospital, I might have said, "Okay, sure." Necessity sometimes obviates one's education. Some of Trump's base felt a necessity when they voted for him. We shall see how many lies and misdeeds it takes before the emperor's nakedness is fully revealed, and fate has its way with him and all of us.

Willing to Be Led Anywhere

MY INITIAL PLAN WAS TO TELL YOU A STORY about my blind date with Liza Minnelli, even though I had told it before in print. I was sure it was an interesting story, and I could spruce it up for this occasion. But to do so almost immediately felt like a laziness, the kind that leads to flatness—the drudgery of each next sentence, old before it gets to its can't-come-soon-enough period, and without the vitality of discovery. I found myself getting bored with myself, and by happenstance drifted off into an altogether different approach; which is largely what follows. Yet a part of me knows that boredom with oneself, compositionally, can be a good thing, an invitation for the imagination to come to the rescue. My real laziness may have been in not seeking ways to invite it. The corollary, of course, is the fallacy of *the interesting subject*, the subject we're so sure is interesting that that becomes its limitation. We just let it unfold, as if it didn't need all of our manipulative skills. The fact was: I was at the beginning of something. My choices were innumerable.

I don't think there are many people likely to be reading this who need to be persuaded that there are many ways to tell a story. To tell it from his perspective or hers, and from what distance, and from what angle of entry—these are some of our obvious options. In my experience, we usually discover the less obvious ones in the act of solving problems. I think it was Donald Barthelme who said that he thought a story should have a beginning, middle, and end, but not necessarily in that order. I suspect he meant the way sometimes our last paragraph or stanza argues to become our first. Or the way a middle becomes a beginning, perhaps after we've invented the middle. And the many ways we fracture and reassemble our stories, and, with the luck that usually comes from skill, manage to cover our tracks.

It's helpful to know we're in the illusion business, that we'll want to make our approximations of reality so compelling and seamless certain readers will simply nod. Much depends on how well we manage time. Our job usually is to slow experience down, to pace and frame it, yet fictionists like García Márquez and Thomas Bernhard sometimes want to speed it up, having written entire books composed of just one long paragraph. Even so, theirs is still a slowed down world going a little faster. A Borges short story, as a further example, might conflate sequences of events, suggesting that to live in the world is to be part of a series of simultaneities. We should hope such contributions to literature are part of our consciousness, but we shouldn't be thinking of them as we write, just as we need to forget that certain readers may be post-structuralists or post-post-structuralists. Better to worry our poems and stories forward, thinking, How do I best get from here to there, and with what phrasing, and what turns. Behind us will be, say, the shards of cubism, various discoveries in physics, jump cuts and angles of vision borrowed from the movies and other media. To keep advancing our subject we need to be ready to make the necessary compromises between our intentions and the in-process discoveries that confound them. This is how to best find the next moment—to listen to what we've put in the air, and to make adjustments accordingly, inspiration being replaced by inspirations, those we've found along the way.

When it comes to closure, depending on our worldview, we might end a story or poem with a definitive click, or with the equivalent of an ellipsis, suggesting that all endings are merely continuations, or new beginnings. Even the definitive click might complete the poem's aesthetic relationships without resolving its human ones. The closure that falsifies experience by slamming the door too tight is simply evidence of the artist failing his subject. In surer hands the slammed door might propel us into a different room.

Formally speaking, the limits to the way a story can be told reside in our ability or inability to give ourselves permission for what we want to do, or what we've found ourselves doing. What are stories and poems anyway, if not artificial arrangements, with chains of interconnections, that suggest purpose and design? Having said that, I know some people would contend that a plotless, idiosyncratic display of mind and sensibility can carry the day—a heady romp with William Gass, for example, or with Djuna Barnes. Well, such romps are also shapely, and have their purposes and designs.

What matters to experienced readers, I suppose, is that in addition to story we sense that the various techniques and styles for telling that story transcend mere trickery, become qualities in and of themselves to look forward to, become part of what constitutes content. We expect the author to perhaps surprise us into our shared humanity, or to make us dream, or even for some good reason to brilliantly break our hearts. In other words, as jazzmen say, to hurt us good, which is another way to please us. Technique, best thought of, is an agent of enchantment and veracity. In the face of true authority—that is, in the presence of sentences and paragraphs that carry built-in tonal assurances that we're in good hands, most of us are willing to be led anywhere.

Poets, especially those who eschew rhyme and meter, may have slightly different ways of demonstrating authority, but their goals—as artificers of the real—are similar. William Carlos Williams, for one, in experiments with syntax and his so-called variable foot, tried to imitate and measure American speech. He wanted the line and the line break to score the poem, to discipline free verse's often mistaken freedoms. George Oppen, someone who learned from Williams, defined syntax as "a careful packing of a poem to avoid a deadening; to avoid destroying a word by its relationships." Both poets were concerned with time and timing—in other words, with rates of disclosure. Like those who followed them—the Olsons, the Creeleys, to the many who sought to seriously play in the field of the page—they wanted to tune and measure how it feels to live in this world. The best free-verse poets are, of course, formalists, which means they demonstrate an intense preoccupation with effects and their orchestration.

Italo Calvino would hold all writers to such compositional standards. "The defects of the clumsy storyteller," he asserts, "are above all offenses against rhythm." Accordingly, when the rhythm is right we, as readers, are most open to the many ways a story can be told. We trust, even relish, delays and obstacles. As in the presence of a good joke teller, we're confident he's enjoying not getting to where he's sure he's going. I might also say how disappointing it can be when authoritative rhythms lead us to moments of vacuity—the equivalent of hearing a punch line that makes us embarrassed for the teller. In such cases, we're likely to resent a skillfulness in service of so little. True authority blends rhythm and voice with subject matter. It has both an inner and an outer melody. I'm thinking in particular of my early experiences with Wallace Stevens, whom I read precognitively for many years. I felt no need to say, "This means . . ." His rhythms and diction sufficiently held me. Over time, those same rhythms led me to his substance, his consequentiality. I trusted the teller long before I understood the tale.

As I said at the outset, my original intention was to tell you a story—an intention that got compromised, nay, lost, almost immediately. You might have liked that story, but midway down the page I found myself remembering Barthelme's comment about beginnings, middles, and ends, which distracted me. I abandoned the Liza story, started with the Barthelme quote, which now, by the way, has found its home in the second paragraph, not the first.

It might be of some interest that my blind date with Liza Minnelli never happened, a fact that seems to always have given me considerable latitude as to choice of detail. Over the years I've added many little touches of verisimilitude. I was prepared to reprise all of them. The blind date, if by this time you're still inclined to trust me, *almost* happened. When I was eighteen or nineteen, some friends asked me if I wanted to go out with Judy Garland's daughter. I said no. Ever since, I've been picking her up at Sutton Place, taking her to the movies. Usually, in most versions, to make the unlikely more credible, I have a lousy time. My audience is rapt, empathetic. The story is driven by what might be called the necessary lie. That is, an illusion in service of what I once considered important: the creation of myself as someone with an interesting life. No such impulse was driving me now. My allegiance is to the poem or the story. I'm just a character in it.

So here you have one of the dangers of "maturity" in a writer—he stops playing, gives up dining out on his Liza story, chooses instead to try to be smart about storytelling without telling a story. Maybe avoidance of what is old news for him gets him somewhere else. It's pretty to think so. But perhaps I should start over. Perhaps, as I implied at the beginning, my imagination was asleep on the job, and my boredom was related to what otherwise should have been thought of as an opportunity: to enliven a half-dead subject. There were, I see now, many options. I could have told the story from Liza's point of view. I could have revealed her essential loneliness, and given myself a scar, and a certain swagger, and, say, a Ford Mustang convertible. Maybe this time we wouldn't have gotten home until the next morning.

George Orwell Sucks

HOW CAN A WORD EVOCATIVE OF SO MUCH PLEASURE, both adult and infantile, find itself used—by almost everybody—in the pejorative? "That really sucks," my friend said after his work was rejected by a journal, or, as I heard last night on television, "As a superstar, he sucks." Several times every day we hear such mindless disapproval. The word has become as debased as the vile "awesome," which is used to suggest approval. "That ice cream is awesome," someone said to me recently, clear evidence that person had never experienced anything like awe, which is a rare phenomenon and tends to make us silent. Have the misusers of "suck" never experienced the delights of sucking or of being sucked? I propose that from here on "He sucks" and "She sucks" be used as words of praise.

The word needs to be restored to the ranks of etymological respectability. Every time we use it, we should be mindful of the various titillations it suggests, or at least of its importance for survival. We tend not to say, "That baby really sucks," but if we did we wouldn't be saying we'd seen a bad baby. We'd merely be referring to what was natural and utilitarian. Even the Puritan in us would approve. We're allowed to suck for survival. It is good for the family and therefore good for the body politic as well. You would think that fact would go some distance toward giving the word a positive connotation.

But it hasn't.

I'm reminded of something Eduardo Galeano wrote: "The church says the body is a sin. The body says: I am a fiesta." Titillation, of course, is in cahoots with disorder, if not chaos. In some ways it's the enemy of the workday. Some of us could suck away an entire week.

My guess is that the pejorative use of sucks stems more from homophobia than from capitalism or our Puritan heritage; in particular, from attitudes toward male homosexuality. To name someone by the epithet that begins with a "c" is much more insulting than to say "he sucks." The "c" word remains taboo in polite conversation. I'd argue that it stems from the historical disgust the culture registers when it imagines two men in the act. Fellatio, by contrast, lacks a certain Anglo-Saxon punch. It sounds Italian, something to enjoy with a good bottle of Barolo. Let us go now, you and I, and commit fellatio under a starry sky. Cops might not want to let on that they know the word. You're unlikely to hear, "Duane, we got us a fellator here, let's run him in."

It's interesting to note that the negative use of sucks has no stigma attached to it. Children say it over dinner. Their parents nod. That cheese soufflé really did suck. The whole family tacitly agrees it was as distasteful as a man sucking another man's penis. Now pass the pasta, Billy.

> "A man may take to drink because he feels himself to be a failure, and then fail all the more completely because he drinks. It is rather the same thing that is happening to the English language. It becomes ugly and inaccurate because our thoughts are foolish, but the slovenliness of our language makes it easier for us to have foolish thoughts."

That's George Orwell, from his 1946 essay "Politics and the English Language." I'm sure Orwell would not want me to say that here in 2018, he'd be turning over in his grave. Literally, I'd have used dead language to indicate that his wisdom has not been heeded. But he might be more upset by the prevalence of foolishness in our thinking than by clichés.

Clichés once had value, even precision. A person who employs them most likely hasn't freshly considered what he is saying, but at least he's chosen something that once was wonderful. After all, "quiet as a mouse" once articulated an aspect of silence. The person who goes around saying this or that sucks not only isn't thinking, he isn't phrasing. I'd call him one of the vulgarizers of language.

I have friends who publicly call people "scumbags," but do not know that a scumbag is a used condom. Almost everyone I know says "cool" about something that they like, thus leveling everything that they like. They make little or no effort to register nuance or gradation. In this way "cool" is as vulgar as the misuse of sucks. It's a scumbag of a word, its user unconscious that he's using something spent.

About such speech, Orwell said,

> "The appropriate noises are coming out of his larynx, but his brain is not involved as it would be if he were choosing his words for himself. . . . he may be almost unconscious of what he is saying, as one is when one utters the responses in church. And this reduced rate of consciousness, if not indispensable, is at any rate favorable to political conformity."

Orwell insisted that language we allow to go unexamined leaves us vulnerable to manipulation by despots and the banality of society-speak. Yet he believed the process was reversible. I'd like to believe so, too. Maybe if I start to hear people say, "That movie sucked. You really have to see it," or "That politician doesn't suck; I don't trust him," then I could start to believe that there's a greater agreement between language and reality, not to mention that the world might be a safer place for sucking, and thus finally more humane.

Dullness and Worry

THE WRITING OF POETRY has had its small-smile moments for me, but more typical feelings after a morning's work (and a good day's work is rarely more than from nine to noon) range from doubt to worry. I'm not complaining. I like doubt and worry; both are propellants, and often lead to discoveries. Certainly their opposite, satisfaction, tends to be in cahoots with stasis. And joy seems to be reserved for those eager to keep their amateur status, a noble wish sometimes, but more often than not a symptom of not having read enough. The highs of inexperience.

So a typical writing day begins by going to my room, putting myself in a place where something might happen. If I find myself beginning a poem, especially one in the first person, I make sure that I'm bored with myself, or at least disinterested. I'm sure I'm not in a poem until the first moment I've startled myself. That is, when language replaces experience as inspiration, and then remains in tension with it throughout the compositional process. And after a while, no matter how authoritative I've been, a *but* is likely to appear; that's how my mind works. I long to write poems that have no *but* in them, that extol without reservation or hate without qualifiers, but with a few exceptions I'm afraid my poems find their energies from counter-drift and dialectic. Sometimes, of course, I sit there like a dummy, dullness leading to dullness. A time to read, perhaps. Or to steal a line from someone smarter than myself, and then try to disguise it. Or to write a letter.

Even on good days, I admit to allowing myself to be interrupted— the phone, the seductions of email. But my favorite mornings are when I work obsessively, when I'm immersed in the problem of the poem. My favorite days are when my working mornings trip over into afternoons and evenings. But even then I'm rarely enthused by what I find myself doing. I'm more inclined to worry it into existence. Maybe, a few weeks later, a quiet satisfaction. Usually followed by doubt.

As Schubert suggests, we all have our sorrows as well as our elations. It's not emotion, but the orchestration of emotion that separates one artist from another. Cold words, finally, like reason, calculation, craft, are the *sine qua non* of my life as a maker of poems. Without them, I could not be successfully passionate.

I always tend to be tinkering, revising. Trench work. I keep digging until I find what I didn't know, or half-knew and didn't yet have the language for. As I said, I like being caught up in the problem or problems of the poem. Behind such tinkering is the conviction that a good poem is a very difficult thing to write.

All in all, a writer's writing life is not very interesting. Behaving badly is often interesting, as is trying to cope with the bad behavior of others, as are most manifestations of wildness. In my studio, I'm the soberest man around, scrupulous and ordinary. I suspect the same is true for most writers. We love syntax more than sin.

Constructions

Musings Toward a Poetics in the Work of Andy Goldsworthy

THE ENGLISH ARTIST/SCULPTOR ANDY GOLDSWORTHY claims to "collaborate with nature." His remarkable work is, in fact, like the best of nature writing. It presents us with acts of consciousness; we see, say, a cluster of fallen leaves and at the same time the unique sensibility that has allowed us to see them. More specifically, in Goldsworthy's case, a sensibility that has arranged them so that we might bring an enlivened eye to what they approximate but aren't exactly. The best nature writing fuses object and language—our noble attempts with a slippery instrument to be as precise as possible. Goldsworthy reconstructs nature. His language, if you will, is nature's fragments—twigs, leaves, stones—transformed into what amounts to a syntax.

The documentary about him, *Rivers and Tides*, is available on Netflix. It gives a fine sense of the man and his work, as does his own Introduction to *Andy Goldsworthy*, the book that contains a wide sampling of photographs of his work. In it, he says, "I take the opportunities each day offers—if it is snowing, I work with snow, at leaf-fall it will be leaves, a blown-over tree becomes a source of twigs and branches. I stop at a place or pick up material by feeling that there is something to discover.... Some places I return to over and over again, going deeper—a relationship in layers over a long time." Listen to a serious artist talk, and there's sure to be compositional resonances into the habits of others artists.

"Nature doesn't fool around," John Ashbery said in one of his art reviews. Indeed, nature may not fool around, but Goldsworthy does fool around with nature. For all his earnestness about his art, there's a high degree of playfulness in it. His so-called "collaboration with nature" is really quite joyous and often perverse, a collaboration of what's there with a sensibility that is powerful, delicate, and nothing if not mischievous. He extracts and abstracts, and in so doing imposes on nature what is inherent in it, until what we're looking at is a semblance of nature. More than anything else, what we're looking at is a Goldsworthy.

He says, "All forms are to be found in nature, and there are many qualities within any material. By exploring them I hope to understand the whole. My work needs to include the loose and the disordered within the nature of the material as well as the tight and regular." Art often makes for strange bedfellows, so one shouldn't be overly surprised when I invoke the writer Henry Miller as an aesthetic comrade of Goldsworthy's. Miller said, "The world has not to be put in order; the world is order incarnate. It is for us to put ourselves in unison with this order." One would imagine that Goldsworthy would approve of such a statement.

Yet with both men, we should trust the tale more than its teller. Miller's way of fulfilling his dicta was often through excess, or what seemed like excess in a time of sexual prudery. In actuality, he was dramatizing, with verve and joy, the pleasures of the body many of us had experienced, but kept to ourselves. Miller's work seemed hyperbolic, even outrageous, because it mimicked sexual indulgence and abandon. Read now, it simply seems accurate. Goldsworthy's art, it can be argued, identifies and highlights for us certain patterns in nature by exaggerating them—his long, winding, snaking walls, for example, or his elemental circles made of dandelions, pinned together with thorns, in the middle of a field. I often find myself smiling at a Goldsworthy creation, the way I smile at Picasso's often wacky virtuosity. Goldsworthy, like Picasso, but unlike Miller, impresses us with delicacy as well as with mass, and with his clean lines. But he is a wonderful exaggerator. We feel in the presence of a structural accuracy, but also a fine excess; both qualities give the work its poetry.

Since I'm citing nonvisual artists in trying to get at Goldsworthy's essence, let me compare him to still another artist working in another art form. Here's what Edwin Denby once said about Balanchine: "George Balanchine is the greatest choreographer of our time. His style is humane because it is based on the patterns the human body makes when it dances; it is not, like romantic choreography—based on patterns the human body cannot quite force itself into."

I would suggest that the artifice employed by both artists involves creating patterns or structures that do not torture or violate the real, but accentuate it. Yeats's famous line, "Who can separate the dancer from the dance?" may apply here. When things go right, yes, we suspend our disbelief. The dancer and the dance fuse. But later our secondary pleasure is in the thinking about how that fusion was achieved. That is, in pondering the way art is *not* like experience, but a fully realized arrangement of gestures and moves, a thing in the world that moments before did not exist. This is my double pleasure with Goldsworthy's work. It intensifies something I recognize, and is an object in its own right.

In the film we see him in the act of making. It's like watching a dance rehearsal, or a scientist in a lab. Some things are tried out, some are retained, some are discarded, or simply collapse. It is in this way that all artists and scientists find their way. The goal is to a fidelity of some sort, a fidelity to shapes in nature, man-made as well as natural, and perhaps shapes that are, in a sense, historical. Goldsworthy's work seems to deliver a tension that exists between the historical and the natural; it will not fully give in to either. Though it tilts toward the underlying patterns in the natural, it also borrows its symmetries and discordances from the history of art and architecture and mythology. We see this in a pyramid of rocks or an arrangement of hollowed-out circles in a field, and in any number of his ice sculptures. Their beauty derives from his surprising execution of what's known by transforming it, using only its natural elements. He defamiliarizes the familiar by invoking it and then doing something else to it—a dead heron's feathers in among stacked branches, to which he adds cut stone, or the addition of a giant snowball, looking moonlike, built onto the bare branches of a tree. Pure mischief. It is beauty happening by the permission he gives himself to construct it.

The man-made object, properly placed in nature, gives the human eye a way of entering the disorderly sprawl. The object collects all that's around it. It changes nothing that is already there. It increases. It focuses.

But I should mention that many of Goldsworthy's creations are designed to go back to nature, not to stand in or apart from it. He photographs their existence as well as their demise. This is fine, but there can be something melodramatic and sentimental when he otherwise draws attention to it, say, by talking about it. The notion of giving back to nature strikes me as precious, especially when you say so as you're showing it to the world. Let the beautiful arrangement of stones disappear when the tide comes in, if that's your plan. Let it be its own testimony. No music coming up, no elbowing. Best to be quiet about our sublimities. Obviously, a small complaint. Goldsworthy's work, whether in place or in the process of vanishing, startles us into reseeing, showing us new ways of regarding what we see.

This was delivered as a talk at a Conference called "The Soul of Beauty" at the University of Houston in November 2006. It has been slightly modified for publication.

Getting a Poem Home

Some Notes about Choreography and Other Arrangements

ONE OF THE PREROGATIVES OF A GUEST EDITOR IS—in the guise of writing an introduction—to address a few pet concerns, then disappear as fast as possible and let my choices do the rest of my speaking for me. So here goes. Paul Valéry famously likened poetry to dancing, prose to walking. I suspect that about each he was half right. Nevertheless, as poets—as I hope is evidenced by the poems in this issue of *Nightsun*—we need to think like choreographers. We must intuit, will, pace, digress, suppress, vary, and arrange—all of which requires a sense of evolving design, and, finally, a form that best serves what ultimately we've found ourselves to be doing.

I imagine the poets in this issue happily struggling with such matters. Their poems, predominantly written in what we loosely call free verse, are dances that must also have been in search of an authenticating music, and thus slowed down, sped up, in the manner of those great trade-offs between a poet's intentions, discoveries, and the textural and sonic demands of the language already in the poem. And this compositional fun was further complicated by the likely fact that their dances were taking place on an open road, a road we can presume was often crooked, with various small paths intersecting it, all full of psychic debris. As they moved forward, they were carrying the baggage of a life lived and of a book-life, the entire history of their reading. So much must have wanted to get into the poem!

Suppression of unruly impulses civilizes a poem, allows its various parts to better cohabit. At best, such suppression—by eliminating the false freedoms of indulgence and solipsism—makes freedom more possible. At worst, it leads to a kind of benignity, the poem so civilized that we'd like to mess up its hair, take it for a joyride. It is the imagination's task to accommodate unruly impulses, to eventually make them feel inevitable. Poems should shimmer with a necessity, or otherwise be "holidays of the mind"—romps for the serious, trips to worlds that resemble ours.

In the presence of a good poem we remember/discover the soul has an appetite, and that appetite is for emotional veracity and for the unsayable. The general condition of my soul, I'm willing to admit, is stoic hunger, stoic loneliness. I'm really only aware of it and its condition when I'm jolted by something surprising or beautiful. Only then do I know what I've been missing. Paul Éluard said, "There is another world, and it is in this one." The very best poems startle us into consideration of that world, and in so doing prick the soul into wakefulness.

In reading for this issue, I will not claim that my soul was always so activated, but the poems I've chosen did engender in me an uncommon alertness. No doubt before these poems reached me they had been arranged and rearranged, worried into a final shape. I was privy only to their virtues, which is what an editor hopes for. If a poem's ending is the home which contains its journey, and a true home is never easily arrived at, I am once again grateful for the dance, the artful walk, and the many other ways in which such difficulty is concealed.

Poetry in a Comsumer Society and the Soul on the Rooftop

MY GUESS WOULD BE that as much as seventy-five percent of the language we encounter in a day is designed to deceive us, or if not exactly to deceive, then to lure us into a purchase. Government-speak aside, our consumer society is in the serious business of using words, not of course to enlighten, but to keep its engine running. I don't mean to suggest a conspiracy. On the contrary, it could be said that this is merely the byproduct of a certain capitalist success story—an optimized marketplace variously dangled before us about which we have the freedom or the delusion of choice. It's a story so successful that even its have-nots, if they were to rebel, likely would be seeking what the haves have. And even those of us capable of asking—Is more less? and, What does it feel like to get what you want and still feel an emptiness?—sometimes find ourselves on the way to the mall in our good cars, albeit foreign ones. I admit to enjoying the great American right of living a bifurcated life, the life of a disdainful participant. It's truly one of our privileges. Yet I often feel like a stranger, a native stranger in a land that doesn't think of itself as strange. I'm always in search, therefore, of language that best serves mixed feelings and the unspoken—the language of poetry. And I always like to find a few compatriots along the way, which is part of my goal tonight.

I'm going to read a few poems that I hope might appeal to you, and thus, with luck, enlarge—by small degree—my feeling of community. No, let me say it more boldly: I'd love to make my taste yours. These poems aren't political, except in the sense that all good poems are corrections of what passes for the true and the conventionally acceptable. If you find them strange, that's their strangeness. They won't exhibit the strangeness of, say, black magic or creatures rising from lagoons or from the dead.

John Ashbery, when asked in an interview why he didn't write poems about the occult, responded, "Because it's not mysterious enough." I

think he meant that being alive in our bodies on any given day is consider-
ably more intriguing. And it is. The poems that address and shape such
mystery frequently end up resembling our lives.

Here's such a poem. It's by Billy Collins.

The Night House

Every day the body works in the fields of the world
Mending a stone wall
Or swinging a sickle through the tall grass—
The grass of civics, the grass of money—
And every night the body curls around itself
And listens for the soft bells of sleep.

But the heart is restless and rises
From the body in the middle of the night,
Leaves the trapezoidal bedroom
With its thick, pictureless walls
To sit by herself at the kitchen table
And heat some milk in a pan.

And the mind gets up too, puts on a robe
And goes downstairs, lights a cigarette,
And opens a book on engineering.
Even the conscience awakens
And roams from room to room in the dark,
Darting away from every mirror like a strange fish.

And the soul is up on the roof
In her nightdress, straddling the ridge,
Singing a song about the wildness of the sea
Until the first rip of pink appears in the sky.
Then, they all will return to the sleeping body
The way a flock of birds settles back into a tree,

Resuming their daily colloquy,
Talking to each other or themselves
Even through the heat of the long afternoons.
Which is why the body—that house of voices—
Sometimes puts down its metal tongs, its needle, or its pen
To stare into the distance,

To listen to all its names being called
Before bending again to its labor.

Why do poets speak in metaphor, and so complicate things? We do it because so much about the world and our participation isn't easily sayable. Some things just can't be said straight out. The motive is not to obfuscate (at least that's true for some of us) but to get closer, memorably, to the actual. Collins, I think, does that in "The Night House" by finding analogues for what he calls "that house of voices," the body. He visualizes for us the restlessness of heart, mind, and soul, which inevitably return to take their places in the body. The poem can be said to approximate our dream lives and how we return from them. It persuades without insistence through invention and delight, and—apropos of my subject tonight—it isn't advertising anything.

Karl Shapiro, in 1960, said that "Advertising is the poetry of the American masses," which still has the ring of the partially true. At its best, advertising makes us aware of things that can enrich or ease our lives, and it also often does so cleverly and delightfully. At its worst, well, it makes us feel stupider than we already are. Whichever, advertising regularly suggests that we can change our lives by the acquisition of things. (Rilke, on the other hand, implies that such change comes from confrontation with self or with beauty.) The fact is that most of us don't want to change a whit. We acquire in order to have more of what will keep us fundamentally the same, or upwardly mobile in a recognizable economic environment. And advertisers, as you know, keep adjusting to what's *au courant*. "Weird," young people tend to say about almost anything that's unfamiliar. Advertisers are so alert to the tendencies of the populace that they've even learned to cater to "weird." It appears that it helps to sell some jeans. Writers who behave equivalently are called hacks. Poets who have an agenda tend to be bad poets.

This is a poem by Mark Strand, a good poet, having some serious fun.

Eating Poetry

Ink runs from the corners of my mouth.
There is no happiness like mine.
I have been eating poetry.

The librarian does not believe what she sees.
Her eyes are sad
and she walks with her hands in her dress.

The poems are gone.
The light is dim.
The dogs are on the basement stairs and are coming up.

Their eyeballs roll,
their blond legs burn like brush.
The poor librarian begins to stamp her feet and weep.

She does not understand.
When I get on my knees and lick her hand,
she screams.

I am a new man.
I snarl at her and bark.
I romp with joy in the bookish dark.

Strand's surreal, hyperbolic dramatization of how one becomes a devourer of poetry, and therefore a little dangerous, is great fun. By eating poetry, the speaker turns into poetry's good dog—a new visceral man, as it were. He snarls, scaring the librarian (that keeper of silence), and is filled with an uncommon joy. Those who haven't romped with joy in the bookish dark are on the rise these days. There are many reasons for this besides the exigencies of capitalism—the speed of the culture, its preoccupation with the visual and the technological—but high among them (and related to them) is that we don't associate contemplation or inwardness with excitement.

Here's a distinctly contemplative poem that primarily employs very direct language, but easily reaches for analogue when the poet feels her subject needs it. It's by Jane Hirshfield.

It Was Like This: You Were Happy

It was like this:
you were happy, then you were sad,
then happy again, then not.

It went on.
You were innocent or you were guilty.
Actions were taken, or not.

At times you spoke, at other times you were silent.
Mostly, it seems you were silent—what could you say?

Now it is almost over.

Like a lover, your life bends down and kisses your life.

It does this not in forgiveness—
between you, there is nothing to forgive—
but with the simple nod of a baker at the moment
he sees the bread is finished with transformation.

Eating, too, is now a thing only for others.

It doesn't matter what they will make of you
or your days: they will be wrong,
they will miss the wrong woman, miss the wrong man,
all the stories they will tell will be tales of their own invention.

Your story was this: you were happy, then you were sad,
you slept, you awakened.
Sometimes you ate roasted chestnuts, sometimes persimmons.

Given the way it starts, it can be argued that the entire poem is a simile for how one might sum up a life. "It was like this," Hirshfield begins, and proceeds to offer a distilled version of a life, elemental and abstract. Those are the terms of the poem; we know early on that we're not going to get many particulars. It wasn't exactly this, it was *like* this. And there are similes within the larger simile. "Like a lover, your life bends down and kisses your life." Followed by another comparison:

It does this not in forgiveness—
between you, there is nothing to forgive—
but with the simple nod of a baker at the moment
he sees the bread is finished with transformation.

Such wonderful matter-of-factness about what is essentially mysterious about a life! It may be that the sophisticated reader might notice that this is a poem written in the second person that feels like a first-person poem, and that the choice of the second person might allow for the speaker's apparently enormous confidence to sound less cocky. That same reader might notice that the pleasure of "persimmons" at the end is prepared for by the consonance and assonance of both "invention" and "awakened." But my guess is that one need not perceive these things for the poem to have appeal.

At the end of a life, the poem says, here's the scoop: Some people may say some things about you, but they'd be wrong. Your life, properly abstracted, was this and this and this. Hirshfield establishes the terms on which she wants her poem to be read, and then pleasingly violates them in her last line. We do not expect concrete nouns like "roasted chestnuts" and "persimmons," but there they are, feeling inevitable and right.

Poems like this one, and there are many which risk speaking so directly, come to us in language that is so eminently clear that even the strange, as in, "your life bends down and kisses your life" feels part of its clarity. This is strangeness normalized by context, and it takes all of Hirshfield's skill to make it feel seamless. Yet I need to remember it's a poem, and poems—no matter their achieved simplicities—are always in danger of feeling like puzzles. It takes experience to get on their wavelengths.

William Carpenter's poem, which I'll read to you now, is written without a single metaphor or simile. It invites us into its what-if world, and asks us to go along for a ride. We go. Its strangeness has behind it, I would argue, much that is familiar to us.

Girl Writing a Letter

A thief drives to the museum in his black van. The night
watchman says Sorry, closed, you have to come back tomorrow.
The thief sticks the point of his knife in the guard's ear.
I haven't got all evening, he says, I need some art.
Art is for pleasure, the guard says, not possession, you can't just
something, and then the duct tape is going across his mouth.
Don't worry, the thief says, we're both on the same side.
He finds the Dutch Masters and goes right for a Vermeer.
"Girl Writing a Letter." The thief knows what he's doing.
He has a Ph.D. He slices the canvas on one edge from
the shelf holding the salad bowls right down to the
square of sunlight on the black and white checked floor.
The girl doesn't hear this, she's too absorbed in writing
her letter. He's already seated at the harpsichord.
He's playing the G Minor Sonata by Domenico Scarlatti,
which once made her heart beat till it passed the harpsichord
and raced ahead and waited for the music to catch up.
She's worked on this letter for three hundred and twenty years.
Now a man's here, and though he's dressed in some weird clothes,

he's playing the harpsichord for her, for her alone, there's no one
else alive in the museum. The man she was writing to is dead—
time to stop thinking about him—the artist who painted her is dead.
She should be dead herself, only she has an ear for music
and a heart that's running up the staircase of the Gardner Museum
with a man she's only known for a few minutes, but it's
true, it feels like her whole life. So when the thief
hands her the knife and says you slice the paintings out
of their frames, you roll them up, she does it; when he says
you put another strip of duct tape over the guard's mouth
so he'll stop talking about aesthetics, she tapes him, and when
the thief puts her behind the wheel and says, drive, baby,
the night is ours, it is the Girl Writing a Letter who steers
the black van on to the westbound ramp for Storrow Drive
and then to the Mass Pike, it's the Girl Writing a Letter who
drives eighty miles an hour headed west into a country
that's not even discovered yet, with a known criminal, a van
full of old masters and nowhere to go but down, but for the
Girl Writing a Letter these things don't matter, she's got a beer
in her free hand, she's on the road, she's real and she's in love.

The uninitiated reader can just have a good zany time with this. A more
experienced reader will likely sense behind the poem a certain bad-boy-
and-girl-in-need-of-being-saved-from-drudgery American romance cli-
ché, into which Carpenter breathes new life. Bonnie and Clyde is there,
as is the roadie novel, and maybe Woody Allen. Carpenter has written like
this before, in his fine book *Rain*. But there are also echoes here of other
contemporary seriocomic fabulists, like poets Stephen Dobyns and Russell
Edson.

In other words, Carpenter pays his debts as he works his territory;
he's both insider and outsider, able to demonstrate his knowledge of art
while exhibiting a kind of frontier mockery of those who would be pomp-
ous about it—the guard in this case, and all that guardianship might imply.
But, while not quite aspiring to satire or parody, he's given us an American
love story in which outlaw high spirits carry the day. Something in our
American collective unconscious makes us unconcerned that the art has

been stolen. Like the girl, we're happy for the temporary liberation from stasis. If we're serious readers of poetry we're equally happy for such well-orchestrated shenanigans.

One of the facts of living in a consumer culture is that memory and its companion, consciousness, are its enemies. (Unless of course what's being sold is based on nostalgia or what it means to be hip.) To remember and value what we already have is to be less susceptible to being persuaded that we need the next doohickey, on which our economy depends. To the extent that poetry might remind us who we are, and perhaps what our true desires are, it's no surprise that poetry isn't considered a useful commodity in the United States. It gets in the way of commerce.

Here's a poem that dramatizes the potential cost of living a life without a consciousness of who we are, but does so delightfully. It's a prose poem, written by David Ignatow, which, as you'll see, introduces us to a man whose life is in grave danger of remaining as is. Ignatow's way of paving the way for the strange is by literary convention. We find ourselves in the more or less comfortable territory of the fable.

(Untitled)

I sink back upon the ground, expecting to die. A voice speaks out of my ear, You are not going to die, you are being changed into a zebra. You will have black and white stripes up and down your back and you will love people as you do not now. That is why you will be changed into a zebra that people will tame and exhibit in a zoo. You will be a favorite among children and you will love the children in return whom you do not love now. Zoo keepers will make a pet of you because of your round, sad eyes and musical bray, and you will love your keeper as you do not now. All is well, then, I tell myself silently, listening to the voice in my ear speak to me of my future. And what will happen to you, voice in my ear, I ask silently, and the answer comes at once: I will be your gentle, musical bray that will help you as a zebra all your days. I will mediate between the world and you, and I will learn to love you as a zebra whom I did not love as a human being.

There's something very beautiful about Ignatow's handling of this, and I urge each one of you to read it out loud so that you can hear and feel it. Who is speaking to this misanthrope? Is it his alter ego, that wiser part of himself, aroused to speak because the man must either change or die? Is it God? Or is it the poet, mediating, as ever, between self and world? What makes it so funny, and so oddly touching, so over-the-top and so fundamentally moral? That's a writer's question as much as it is a reader's.

I suggest to those of us who write that it's relatively easy to get into a little invention like this one, but difficult to get out of it. Ignatow brilliantly uses the refrain, both as musical device and moral emphasizer. But what I admire most are the two turns that he makes. Most short poems can afford only one turn, and most poets would have been content with this: "All is well, then, I tell myself silently, listening to the voice in my ear speak to me of my future." In a person we thought would be resistant to change, the metamorphosis has already started to take place. It's as if he said to himself, "Sure, a zebra, that makes sense. Already I feel more compassionate than ever." This is funny, but also acts as evidence of what can happen when one is finally able to listen to the right voice. But Ignatow goes one step further, allowing the speaker to worry about what will happen to the voice, then allowing that voice to tell us. We see that the voice itself, through its own transformative powers, also has been made more loving.

If we write our poems with our second selves, as Dave Smith claims we do, isn't this poem emblematic of how a poet inhabits his own poem? Transforming, mediating, shaping. As in the previous poems, the author's spirit and intellect are everywhere present. They're part of what we're listening to as we listen. That is, of course, the more we get in the habit of listening. This is a poem that perhaps should be encountered midway in a semester, or midway in a life.

I want to conclude with a poem by Brigit Pegeen Kelly about which I'll say little. It's something to devour, which I give to you without napkin or the comfort of paraphrase. In fact I'm hoping that it will leave you, as some of the very best poems do, somewhat inconsolable. I don't think there's anything to interpret.

Song

Listen: there was a goat's head hanging by ropes in a tree.
All night it hung there and sang. And those who heard it
Felt a hurt in their hearts and thought they were hearing
The song of a night bird. They sat up in their beds, and then
They lay back down again. In the night wind, the goat's head
Swayed back and forth, and from far off it shone faintly
The way the moonlight shone on the train track miles away
Beside which the goat's headless body lay. Some boys
Had hacked its head off. It was harder work than they had imagined.
The goat cried like a man and struggled hard. But they
Finished the job. They hung the bleeding head by the school
And then ran off into the darkness that seems to hide everything.
The head hung in the tree. The body lay in the tracks.
The head called to the body. The body to the head.
They missed each other. The missing grew large between them,
Until it pulled the heart right out of the body, until
The drawn heart flew toward the head, flew as a bird flies
Back to its cage and the familiar perch from which it trills.
Then the heart sang in the head, softly at first and then louder,
Sang long and low until the morning light came up over
The school and over the tree, and the singing stopped....
The goat had belonged to a small girl. She named
The goat Broken Thorn Sweet Blackberry, named it after
The night's bush of stars, because the goat's silky hair
Was dark as well water, because it had eyes like wild fruit.
The girl lived near a high railroad track. At night
She heard the trains passing, the sweet sound of the train's horn
Pouring softly over her bed, and each morning she woke
To give the bleating goat his pail of warm milk. She sang
Him songs about girls with ropes and cooks in boats.
She brushed him with a stiff brush. She dreamed daily
That he grew bigger, and he did. She thought her dreaming
Made it so. But one night the girl didn't hear the train's horn.
And the next morning she woke to an empty yard. The goat
Was gone. Everything looked strange. It was as if a storm

Had passed through while she slept, wind and stones, rain
Stripping the branches of fruit. She knew that someone
Had stolen the goat and that he had come to harm. She called
To him. All morning and into the afternoon, she called
And called. She walked and walked. In her chest a bad feeling
Like the feeling of the stones gouging the soft undersides
Of her bare feet. Then somebody found the goat's body
By the high tracks, the flies already filling their soft bottles
At the goat's torn neck. Then somebody found the head
Hanging in a tree by the school. They hurried to take
These things away so that the girl would not see them.
They hurried to raise money to buy the girl another goat.
They hurried to find the boys who had done this, to hear
Them say it was a joke, a joke, it was nothing but a joke....
But listen: here is the point. The boys thought to have
Their fun and be done with it. It was harder work than they
Had imagined, this silly sacrifice, but they finished the job,
Whistling as they washed their large hands in the dark,
What they didn't know was that the goat's head was already
Singing behind them in the tree. What they didn't know
Was that the goat's head would go on singing, just for them,
Long after the ropes were down, and that they would learn to listen,
Pail after pail, stroke after patient stroke. They would
Wake in the night thinking they heard the wind in the trees
Or a night bird, but their hearts beating harder. There
Would be a whistle, a hum, a high murmur, and, at last, a song,
The low song a lost boy sings remembering his mother's call.
Not a cruel song, no, no, not cruel at all. This song
Is sweet. It is sweet. The heart dies of this sweetness.

Am I right in believing that the strangeness of this poem is no impediment to the understanding of it? The poem exists in the valley of its making. It's not trying to sell us a thing.

We've had a little tête-à-tête tonight here in one of our refuges, a college, one of those places where such talks can take place. Outside, when we leave, there'll be WalMart and MacDonald's, Macy's, and Home Depot.

They'll be calling to us, and few of us will resist. Their song is not as sweetly damning as the song of the goat's head to the boys, though it would be useful for us to surmise that by its existence it's a consumer culture song, hear it as such, then make our decisions accordingly. I, too, like my double cheeseburgers and bargain prices, not to mention big, comfortable couches and luxuries I could do without. But I can't help but remember Billy Collins's "The Night House" in which "the soul is up on the roof / In her nightdress, straddling the ridge." Collins had something else in mind, but I'm writing about poetry in a consumer culture, and I'm worried about that soul. Maybe the soul is evoked because it's hasn't been spoken to for months, even years, and is lonely. Maybe it's only heard "Buy this" or "Buy that." Maybe it feels like jumping from that ridge.

In countries where scarcity is the rule and basic freedoms are suppressed, poetry is that much more valued, and more regularly has the feel of the necessary, the urgent. Our luck and bane is to be largely protected from such urgencies. I say largely because for sure the impoverished and variously excluded from the success story have reason to feel otherwise. Still, to find answers or solace through poetry is a rarity. The major exception was the immediate aftermath of 9/11 when the need for poetry seemed to measurably increase, the populace craving articulation for the chaos of its feelings, the chaos of the moment. Commerce, for a while, took a back seat. The soul—dare I say the American soul?—almost was visible, so much so that some of us knew that nothing we could give it would ever be enough. I, for one, for reasons I can't yet articulate, never felt more strangely alert.

Play and Seriousness

The Secret Code the Student Thinks the Teacher Knows,
and Other Impediments to Loving Poetry

I'M PLEASED TO BE HERE in Minnesota today for several reasons, but primarily because it is here where my teaching career began. In 1971 I was hired by Southwest Minnesota State College, located on the prairie in Marshall. Philip Dacey and Howard Mohr were hired at the same time, and though I returned east after three years, and they stayed, we remain friends to this day. Minneapolis was where I first taught in the Poetry in the Schools program sponsored by The Arts Council, directed by the wonderful Molly LaBerge. I must admit I began visiting K-12 classrooms without any messianic zeal, but to make a little more money than Southwest was able to pay me. But my motives weren't entirely mercenary. At that time, I was delighted that anyone believed I was a poet, and would refer to me as one.

Though much has changed in the schools since I first started teaching over forty years ago, I think I can address the teaching of poetry—that bad, often neglected boy of the curriculum—which seems to always need a push and a shove from somewhere or someone. So today I'm going to try to be one of those someones, and dare to be somewhat pedagogically subversive about the subject.

There must be many of you in the audience who don't need a push and a shove, and if you are among them, then make believe I'm speaking to some of your recalcitrant friends or administrators, those folks (and I was one of them once) for whom poetry never quite touched or informed. I was one of those students who thought poetry was written in code, a code your teachers knew and you didn't, and if you managed to break the code you got an A. I need not say that such an approach to poetry does not inspire any love of it. And I'm sure that some of you, educated that way, have taught poetry in such a manner. So today I'd like to offer a few suggestions as to how the teaching of poetry might be improved, perhaps even made joyful.

Coleridge said that poetry must entertain before it can instruct, and I'd like to start with that as a given.

Of course, "entertainment," for some people, can mean pulling the wings off of lightning bugs, or watching pro wrestling, while for others it might be spending evenings mastering the pronunciation of the names of French critics. Let's agree not to be specific, and let's, for a while, think of poetry as that which produces a heightened alertness. An alertness to what? To the world around us, to ourselves, to language itself and what Wallace Stevens calls its sudden rightnesses. Pleasure is what most of us want from our reading experiences, though I would include well-rendered evocations of suffering and hardship among my pleasures. (In that regard I should mention that Ingmar Bergman films that others thought depressing, elated me, the way excellence elates.) At any rate, I'd like to amend Coleridge's statement by saying that poetry need not instruct, the way a beautiful bowl or a Picasso painting need not instruct. There are, of course, many poetries, from "Jabberwocky" to *The Waste Land* and, like Bergman films and cubist Picassos, that speak to, depict, and enlarge the varieties of human experience.

As a poet in the schools, I had a variety of duties, some days with the very young, some with hormone-driven 7th and 8th graders. But I had the advantage of having poet Kenneth Koch's book *Wishes, Lies, and Dreams,* with its wonderful exercises and prompts. His "lies" exercise always produced the most interesting work. Tell a lie about almost anything, and you get something either closer to the truth, or a phrase or two that would lead to other seminal language. "Tell three lies about school," I recall, worked particularly well. A 6th grader wrote, "Naked teachers grade freely and easily" as one of his three. His classmates loved it, as did I, but his teacher was a little abashed.

That's a prompt I don't think I can give in today's touchy and litigious climate. Sometimes not even then, but I learned it was useful to hold a workshop for the teachers before I'd enter a classroom. I'd tell them that I wasn't encouraging their students to be liars. The prompt was designed to give students permission to make things up, to use their imaginations. The illusion that they were doing something illicit was also energizing. I'd say this, and hope for the best. So one way to get students to like poetry is to have them write it, and to read it out loud to the class. But the lines they write need to startle, often be outrageous. They laugh. They moan *ah ahs*. A good prompt will impel them out of the conventional.

Having fun with language is the first point when it comes to getting kids to write poems. An inner city 4th grader in New Jersey wrote his three lies about spring:

> In spring the ice cream man faints.
> In spring everybody turns into stamps.
> In spring rotten birds fly for air.

The third lie was usually the best, as is the case here. But the other students liked all—a relief, I guess, from the usual spate of daffodil poems, genteel and polite, that they had been exposed to. A poet needed to startle or surprise, be a contrarian. You could even be funny! Before we'd begin, I'd say that I didn't expect whole poems from them, but rather interesting moments. Poems are built on a series of interesting moments, and we shouldn't expect whole poems from young people not named Keats or Rimbaud. Instead, tell some lies about your body. Where does your shadow go when you go to sleep at night? Where does the dark come from? I'd try to give them prompts that would stir the imagination. Done in the right spirit, the results usually are rather easy to praise; some, of course, more than others. Once praised, the students tend to be braver and eager to do more. I must brag a little, and tell you what my ten-year-old daughter wrote in response to Where does the dark come from? "The dark comes from the weakness of the infinity of numbers." It was, to this day, the smartest thing she ever said, but of course neither she nor I had any idea what it means.

I realize that I'm addressing a wide range of people today with different curriculum needs, and standards you must not only reach, but uphold. State tests that you must teach toward. Issues of security must both distract and need to be dealt with. If I have an advantage, it is that I'm an outsider without your commitments, and so have a chance of telling a few minor truths. So far I've been talking about playing with language and the usefulness of having students write poetry before and while they are reading it.

One caution before I proceed: try not to ask them to write directly about important subjects. For example, themselves. Try not to be interested in their feelings. Be their teacher, not their shrink. Their feelings will manifest more interestingly if they're talking about a wish they have, or in describing a tree. Their personal revelations, perhaps interesting as information, are usually linguistically boring. They need to find their important subject, which can be small, and keep finding it. To start with it, well, there's a likelihood they'll merely carry out their original intention, and discover nothing in the doing. Besides, you're all English teachers, not psychologists. You can be of more use to your minions by correcting their syntax than by learning about their sins or how they've been sinned against.

May I also suggest that you begin your poetry units by reading minor poems that you love. Your enthusiasm for the art is as important as anything you might say about it. Your enthusiasm confers value. One way to think of poetry is that it's a conversation between self and world. The best poets arrange their poems so that conversation can be overheard. With comic poems, the same thing is true. Remember that the comic often slides into the serious, and vice versa. How then to teach a poem? Remember that diction, rhythm, texture are part of what a poem means. Read the poem out loud. If you do, there's a better chance they will hear its tone or tones. Read it with pleasure. Accentuate the moments you think are more important than others.

As English teachers, it is important for us to keep in mind some of the clear statements poets have made about poetry and the imagination. One of my favorites is W.H. Auden's, "Poetry is the clear expression of mixed feelings." Here are some others.

"The same people will be apt to take poems right as know how to take
a hint when there is one and not to take a hint when none is intended."
　　—Robert Frost

"The power of the mind over the possibilities of things."
　　—Wallace Stevens on Imagination

"The best words in the best order."
—Samuel Coleridge

"Expressing oneself is saying what one doesn't feel"
—Fernando Pessoa

The Pessoa quote deserves at least an essay in itself. Suffice it to say for now that many poems and marriages would be improved if that were general knowledge.

But given my subject today, Robert Frost's aphorism about poetry is perhaps most apt: "If it is with outer seriousness, it must be with inner humor. If it is with outer humor, it must be with inner seriousness." Frost is more sly than funny. For your high school age students, choose to study, say, "Mending Wall," or "The Road Not Taken," two poems of his that appear simple, yet are easy to misread. To read them well requires acute attention to detail.

I recommend teaching your students to be as humble as is possible before a text. This might mean that their early take on a poem might have to be abandoned because, say, lines eight and nine seem to be pointing in a different direction. I have a friend who seems incapable of altering his first sense of a poem. He always clings to whatever his first impulse was, and proceeds to cite as evidence for his mistake lines that have gone elsewhere. The poem before him will always be about failed love because, say, in the second line the speaker indicated some form of marital disappointment. That the poem has moved on to other concerns, like airstrikes in Syria, or walk-off home runs in Yankee Stadium, doesn't seem to matter to him. He continues to see the poem through the lens of marital discord. Let's call him the stubborn bad reader.

Another type might be the reader generally unaware that a poem or a poet, through arrangement, will be suggesting a certain strategy of presentation. This is the kind of reader we might call the literalist, often tone deaf, who will miss authorial hints. In "Mending Wall," for example, Frost tempts us to think one slogan is truer than another. The good reader senses "Good fences make good neighbors" and "Something there is that doesn't love a wall" are both true, even though one of the protagonists has considered his position more thoroughly than the other.

Nevertheless, the reader always completes the poem; it's inevitable. Perhaps the writer can control one level of meaning, and maybe a second resonance as well. Beyond that, who knows? I want my readers at the least to make a gesture toward the words I've used and the order I've used them in. Sometimes, of course, the reader perceives what the writer has not, and enlarges the poem's subject, informs the poet.

Good readers, I think, are a rare breed these days. In the world according to Dunn, here are some of their qualities: they believe the author is not just a product of his social and political times, but a maker, a creator of systems of language that bear on our lives. They have read or heard about the Deriridas, the Lacans, the Foucaults, and therefore have confronted that language is a series of signs, that it supposedly only refers to itself, that it is inexact, indeterminate, and—if they believe that—I would want their task as readers to be all the more careful, and to know that precise approximations of the real are an achievement, perhaps the best that language can offer. They've learned to deconstruct a text, but if they are smart they know that's just one way of interpreting a poem. My favorite readers know that the author is not dead, that the burden of the reader is to bring his or her full intelligence to the occasion. It would also be useful if they've read Aristotle, Maritain, Wordsworth, Strunk, Pound, Virginia Woolf, Stevens, Empson, T.S. Eliot, Kenneth Burke, Katherine Anne Porter, Randall Jarrell, E.B. White, William Gass, Paul Valéry, to name just a few who write great sentences and have something to say on the subject. Even these notables have many biases, which they bring to the reading of a text. It's important that we all have some cognizance of our own.

To read well you have to know yourself well, your tics and your tendencies, the subjects on which you're most likely to err. One of the useful things you can do for your (older) students is to allow yourself to be publicly wrong. Show the students how easy it is to misread, or half-read a poem, or that the poem in question allows, maybe intends, multiple interpretations. Talk about what you missed in early readings of the poem. Perhaps how reading it out loud, or attempting an exegesis of it, made you aware of what was not otherwise readily available to you. Or the students did.

A good poem to discuss might be Theodore Roethke's "My Papa's Waltz."

My Papa's Waltz

The whiskey on your breath
Could make a small boy dizzy;
But I hung on like death:
Such waltzing was not easy.

We romped until the pans
Slid from the kitchen shelf;
My mother's countenance
Could not unfrown itself.

The hand that held my wrist
Was battered on one knuckle;
At every step you missed
My right ear scraped a buckle.

You beat time on my head
With a palm caked hard by dirt,
Then waltzed me off to bed
Still clinging to your shirt.

Some students are disposed to read this as an angry poem. I then suggest that they try to read it as a father-son ritual, a mixture of drunken roughhousing and affection. Which reading holds up? Why? The class usually divides on this. I point to the phrasing and the tone, and suggest that different, stronger language would be used if Roethke were writing a poem about child abuse. "We romped" suggests playfulness and fun. Yes, the mother disapproves, but only with a frown. And the title suggests a kind of romantic, elegant dance, even if it's used ironically. The counter argument is the use of "death" in the first stanza, the scraping of the boy's ear, the beating time on his head. It's not easy to explain away those choices, though I've tried on occasion, but have found myself having to yield to the possibility of dual tones in the poem, and to the essential ambiguity of the event. Roethke's various revisions of the poem are suggestive of this ambiguity. (I'll not cite them here for reasons of time.) But I remind my students that this poem was written in 1948 and they (the students of today) are quicker to think of child abuse and the dangers of drunkenness in such a "dance," as opposed to a kind of roughhousing that leads to filial connection. ". . . waltzed me off to bed / Still clinging to his shirt." Many won't buy this historical positioning, and I'm content to leave it at that. As I said earlier, the reader completes the poem.

But my subject today is the many ways playfulness can lead to seriousness, and though in some ways "My Papa's Waltz" bridges the two, let me offer some poems, or rather lines of poems by children, that I would suggest you read to other children before beginning any unit on poetry. As you'll see, they demonstrate that imagination wedded to experience is the stuff of poetry, and can be arrived at through play, and often through the arbitrary as well. After reading some poems as set up, I should mention I give the students no more than ten minutes to write.

Here's a response from a 2nd grade girl to an "If I were . . . then I would" exercise. She spoke it:

> If I was a bat as dark as the sky
> I would fly up real high
> past midnight

What follows is a collaborative 2nd grade poem based on wishes:

> I wish my shadow was like my conscience
> and in the middle of the morning
> it went down with the moon
> and came up with the sun
> and started all over again

And a 4th grader's response to lies about his shadow:

My shadow is an old man
from my other life
who hangs around on sunny days

And this, my favorite, also a 6th grader's: The saddest thing:

The saddest thing I ever saw was a daisy
with black and pink spots.
The yellow thing in the middle was blue.

Here's an exercise for older students, though I imagine it might work with younger ones as well. Ask students to write down three objects that a hunter uses and three that are related to carpentry. Or objects that a cook might use and three that are related to carpentry. (Carpentry has so many maker's tools, it always works well). Then they are to exchange what they've written with another classmate. They then must write a poem that is neither about hunting or carpentry, or cooking and carpentry. I give them optional first lines, "There are no paths left anymore." And "If you do not stir, no one will find you."

Here are two poems, both using the first prompt, and both from 10th graders:

There are no paths left anymore—
anywhere.
There are no birds left anymore
to watch or pick
at their orange coats.
There are no dogs left
that haven't heard
the sound of a strong gun—
because a skillful ruler
wound up his toy men,
gave them lumber
and put
a hammer and some nails
in their hands.

They built an entire square
of tall buildings
with bright lights.
They created smog and crime
and built a heaven
only for themselves.

*

There are no paths left anymore.
The mean one with the gun and the knife,
and the young one with the hammer and nails
came. The trees are gone—boards for the houses.
The animals are gone—they followed the decoy to the gun.

And two poems that were inspired by Etheridge Knight poems
that I read to a 12th grade class:

My poems are lovely
They blossom in the dark
rooms of loneliness . . .

*

Poems could make you feel happy
on a rainy day like this
Poems are not cool
If you not cool you can't understand the poem
Poems are about the system of yourself

With the possible exception of the last two poems, I would argue
that the claims this grouping of poems makes would *not* be as surprisingly
good if the students were asked to say something that mattered to them
about their lives. The trick is to convince them (by following the arbitrary
dictates of the prompts) that they are more likely to say something interest-

ing, and often truer than if they tried to be meaningful. But you don't have to convince them. What they end up writing usually proves the point.

To play our way into seriousness is often to disarm our inner critic—that man or woman we've cultivated to legislate our excesses. Play has a way of slipping in the side door. Suddenly we're in a room, with only ourselves to stop us. Play of course can lead to frivolity or silliness, what Coleridge in his *Biographia Literaria* calls fancy. There's nothing to stop us from inventing the next thing. Fancy, I would maintain, is not injurious to the imagination of the young writer. Let him have unsupervised play. But Coleridge elevates the imagination over the fanciful because it has cohering properties; it will not let us go on and on. I prefer poems that exhibit the eros of moral complexity, poems that slow down enough to allow us to examine their subject, like "My Papa's Waltz," or, say, "Prufrock." I love "Jabberwocky" too, and poems that brilliantly derange the senses. But usually history and the dialectics of literary aesthetics take care of that for us: one movement reacting to the other, naturalism reacting to romanticism, the advent of free verse feeling liberating, radical, then becoming indulgent, sloppy, followed by a wish for greater discipline, greater formalities, etc.

I'll conclude with an image and statement from a famous writer, who has earned the right to make such a claim. And a playful poem by a girl, written in less than ten minutes. The first came out of years of experience, the second out of the nowhere of a playful imagination.

"Soft water eats hard stone; let someone else make it rhyme."
　　　　—José Saramago

There was once a box of boys.
The box brought pleasure to all girls.
Once a girl found a box of boys.
Most of these boys were cute. I was
really having fun until a bunch
of girls with wings came flying by.
　　　　　—Lyn R, 8th grade

3

Sports and Art

*Acceptance Speech given after being inducted
into the International Scholar/Athlete Hall of Fame*

I SEE MY INDUCTION into the Scholar/Athlete Hall of Fame as one of the most satisfying honors that's ever been bestowed on me. It fuses the two aspects of my life to which I've given the most time and dedication: sports and poetry, though I must say that my accomplishments as a basketball player needed a lot of help from my poetry to enable me to be so honored tonight. I was a decent basketball player who had the great fortune of playing on excellent teams. There are records to prove both. Pretty difficult to say the shot went in when it didn't, though I'm sure many of us—with the smokescreen of time and with help from our needy imaginations—have told stories of our exploits that are slightly enlarged. Sometimes it helps not to have been famous, to have led a life somewhat below the radar. But if the paper the next morning says you shot 0 for 14, you can't very easily say you had a good night. Here's one thing that differentiates sports and art: by degree, you can get away telling more lies about yourself if you're an artist. A poet can argue, for example, that he's ahead of his time or just plain misunderstood. In other words, that bad review which said, in effect, that none of his shots went in, simply was defining "shots" too narrowly, couldn't see that alternate universe where they swished and slam-dunked. There's no poet's box score, and if there were there'd be no universal agreement on what the figures meant.

I'm being too reductive, I know. I'm just trying to say thank you for overlooking some things, emphasizing others. After all, to be an athlete or an artist is to live with failure, if not the likelihood, then certainly the possibility of it. And whatever our successes we know that they almost immediately ask to be replicated; we're already thinking *what next*. The pleasures we feel and enjoy are intertwined with the difficulties of earning them. To be an athlete or an artist is to put yourself out there where you'll be judged. That's why the fan who boos failure—as opposed to lack of effort—is a coward. He risks nothing for his kicks. This is true of some critics, too. I love excellence. I assume all of us do. But on the way to excellence are often noble failures. The good fan and the good critic know something about them.

I want to refer to a pastiche of things tonight that will directly and indirectly speak to some of the above. I'll start with a poem that has as an epigraph a quote from Albert Camus:

Lucky

> Loyal obedience to the rules jointly defined and freely accepted.
> —*Albert Camus, on why his only true lessons*
> *in morality came from sports.*

Lucky that we didn't know the games we played
    were teaching us about boundaries
and integrity; it would have smacked of school,

we who longed for recess. And lucky—when exiled
    to right field, or not chosen at all—
we didn't know the lesson was injustice,

just how much of it we could tolerate.
    But always there'd be the boys
who never got it, calling foul when foul

there wasn't, or marking with an X the spot
    where the ball didn't hit.
Where are they now? What are they doing?

Lucky that some of us who loved recess
    came to love school,
found the books that gave us a few words

for what the aggrieved already knew. Lucky
    that within rules
freely accepted we came to recognize a heart

can be ferocious, a mind devious and yet fair.

And here's another:

Competition

Because he played games seriously
    and therefore knew grace
comes hard, rises through the cheap

in us, the petty, the entire history
    of our defeats,
he looked for grace in his opponents,

found a few friends that way
    and so many others
he could never drink with, talk to.

He learned early never to let up,
    never to give
a weaker opponent a gift

because so many times he'd been
    that person
and knew the humiliation in it,

being pandered to, a bone for the sad
    dog. And because
he remembered those times

after a loss when he'd failed
        at grace—
stole from the victor

the pleasures of pure victory
        by speaking
about a small injury, or the cold

he wasn't quite over—he loved
        those opponents
who'd shake hands and give credit,

save their true and bitter stories
        for their lovers, later,
when all such lamentations are comic,

the sincere if onlys of grown men
        in short pants.
Oh there were people who thought

all of it so childish; what to say to them,
        how to agree,
ever, about dignity and fairness?

I see now, in typing out these poems (written many years apart) that both of them end on words like "fair" and "fairness." We who've played sports know how quickly character is revealed in a game, and the importance of the way one demonstrates (or doesn't) that quality. As I indicate in the second poem, I've known within minutes whether I'd like to have a social relationship with my fellow competitor, and deeply regret the times I've revealed my own shortcomings in this regard.

It's why, generally, short story writers establish a moment of crisis early on in their stories—the better the opportunity to examine character as the plot unfolds. Anyone can be decent and fair-minded when the sun is out and equanimity abounds. It's that much more difficult in the midst and heat of trying to win a point. And more difficult still when you've won a point with a great shot (fill in the sport of your choice) and your opponent sulks and blames it on himself.

Hemingway coined the term "grace under pressure" and used bull fighting to illustrate what he meant. He thought you could tell a lot about a man by how he fought the bull, and of course you can—a lot, but not enough. A bad bullfight in Spain is a disgusting spectacle, a little less disgusting in Mexico where the bull is not killed. And even the "good" fights are unfair. In Camus' terms, the bull hasn't freely chosen to participate. Nevertheless, if one's major criterion for judging the worth of a man is in how he behaves when faced with danger, then Hemingway's extreme example of the bullfight carries some weight. I've seen a great torero, Paco Camino, in action, and that action was slow and balletic, his cape work artful, his proximity to the bull so close that I felt an almost unbearable witnessing. The parallel Hemingway makes in *The Sun Also Rises* is to writing—the clean line, the precision, the gutsiness of working close to your subject, etc. But there's more to a man than how he exhibits courage, even more to a man whose artfulness is so fine we may find ourselves forgiving what in others we might condemn. Excellence seems to have its privileges.

Tonight I feel honored to be here, and only somewhat worthy. I haven't come off the ropes in the 8th round and knocked out George Foreman, nor have I risked a prison sentence for speaking my convictions. I've won a game or two with a last second shot, but have never been close to being Jordanesque. I haven't been the greatest or even the best in any field. But I have had what athletics and poetry writing can offer: moments of transcendence. On a few given days, I've been better than myself, found myself on the basketball court unable to miss, or in my studio writing things I didn't know I knew. And then it was back to the mundanities of living. My accomplishments have gotten me in this door, in this Hall, and I'm grateful and humbled to be among a few peers and my many superiors.

Introduction to E.E. Cummings Complete Poems

LIKE MANY POETS OF MY GENERATION, I've had for years an on-again, off-again love affair with Cummings. It began in my early twenties when I was wrestling with seriousness and playfulness and the sensual and wanting all three braided and linked in a poem. Cummings was high on my list of poets who seemed able to combine these qualities. I knew, however, that among my contemporaries, Eliot, Stevens, and William Carlos Williams, as well as a few others, were held in higher esteem than was Cummings.

The problem for me was that I understood little of Eliot and even less of Stevens. And though Williams was a sensualist and a revolutionary, whom I thought I understood, whose favorite flower was saxifrage, a weed "that splits the rocks," he was also a poet in search of a quintessential American idiom. As such, he was an integral figure, as were Eliot and Stevens, in the great modernist enterprise. Cummings was on the periphery. His sonnets, for example, were typographically revolutionary, yet they were sonnets. Ezra Pound's admonition to "make it new" seemed to point toward a different newness and to poems that demanded more of the reader. But there's a playful, ironic toughness to many of Cummings' poems, the sonnets included. Witness "next to of course god america" and "pity this busy monster, manunkind," which ends with "we doctors know / a hopeless case if—listen: there's a hell / of a good universe next door: let's go".

It's hard to imagine Berryman's *Dream Songs* without Cummings' experiments with syntax preceding them. And if he doesn't achieve the authoritative power of the high modernists, his poems regularly demonstrate what one critic called "a subversive smallness," which is no small thing.

I'm taken by the speed of his poems, too, and how that speed—often enforced by compounded words and sentences with frolicking syntax—rarely, for all such hijinks, sacrifices clarity. The poem that begins

Buffalo Bill's
defunct
    who used to
    ride a watersmooth-silver
                stallion
and break onetwothreefourfive
pigeonsjustlikethat

is one such example.

If Eliot thought that "April is the cruellest month" and Williams wrote "Lifeless in appearance, sluggish / dazed spring approaches" and Stevens in "Sunday Morning" delivered the fertile lushness of a heaven on earth, I admit to being more charmed at the time by Cummings' description of spring as "mud-luscious" and "puddle-wonderful."

But therein lies my dilemma. I still love "mud-luscious" but have come to understand that April is cruel because it promises growth and an end to sluggishness. And here we are—in the beautiful thick of it—occasionally feeling dazed, or baffled by desire, or unfulfilled. Mud-luscious and puddle-wonderful, by comparison, are lightweight fun.

But I don't wish to dwell on such a small aspect of his oeuvre. Edward Estlin Cummings, 1894–1962, was born in Cambridge, Massachusetts, the son of a Unitarian minister who also taught sociology at Harvard. The poet himself received a B.A. and an M.A. from Harvard and, in 1916, volunteered to go to France as a member of the Norton-Harjes Ambulance Corps. This led to some difficulties with a French censor over certain letters he had written, thought to be subversive, and he was interned for three months in a concentration camp. His semifictional book *The Enormous Room* came out of that experience. He was married twice, both for short periods, but lived with his common-law wife, Marion Morehouse, a photographer, from 1934 until his death.

After the war, Cummings lived in Paris, writing and painting. His first full-length book of poems, *Tulips and Chimneys*, appeared in 1923, one year after—it should be noted—Eliot's *The Waste Land* and Joyce's *Ulysses*, two books that Pound championed into print. *Tulips and Chimneys* was distinguished by a contrarian charm; it had no comparable champion.

Cummings was one of America's great technical innovators, an iconoclastic opponent of convention, power, and hypocrisy—and a very fine poet. In graduate school, however, I succumbed to the prevailing estimate of his work, relegating him to minor status. I allowed myself to fall out of love with him. But to reread him now is to find many old pleasures. Minor and major are often slippery, not to mention nasty, designations, and it seems important not to turn our backs on those who have given us such originality, wit, and pretty how towns.

My most embarrassing teaching moment, in fact, occurred while teaching "anyone lived in a pretty how town." I had never taught before and was given an Intro to Literature class to publicly display my insecurity and ignorance. I read the poem to the class, pronouncing *noon*e as *none* all the way through. When I finished, a young woman raised her hand and said, "Mr. Dunn, isn't that *noon*e (two syllables), not *none*?" I instantly knew she was correct and said, "No, that's *none* who lived in a pretty how town" and never changed my opinion the entire semester. I think of that incident whenever I find a reader misreading a poem of mine. I can neither forgive that reader nor myself for our carelessness, though I know that in every (often infuriating) instance, the reader completes the poem.

I still love the lyrical exuberance of that poem, its refrain and twists of syntax, as I continue to love "my father moved through dooms of love" and the sexual comedy in "may i feel said he." His more satirical poems like "i sing of Olaf glad and big" and "the Cambridge ladies who live in furnished souls" tend to have their maximum impact on first reading, whereas the love poems invite return after return.

Cummings is the Holden Caulfield of American poetry. What he loves doesn't change as he gets older, and the impurities and phoniness he encounters are attacked with the same youthful innocence. Yet his spontaneity and diction and rhythms are noble and contagious. After reading him, I'd like to walk around Cambridge or Paris with him, sharing in his enthusiasms and his disapprovals. Milan Kundera once described the lyric poet as the poet of inexperience. I believe he meant it as a compliment.

How many of us can retain our wonderment at what we see and feel? And for how long? Cummings did it for over twenty years. And he did it with a memorable formal dexterity, a new way to arrange and frame experience on a page.

My New Jersey

IT WOULDN'T EXACTLY BE CORRECT TO SAY that New Jersey has inspired my work, though I lived in southern New Jersey for thirty years. For almost twenty of those years, details with a New Jersey tint would trickle into poems, but so did, of course, the sky. Like other aspects of my environment, it was there while I worried and ate and did chores. It was simply available. I'd find myself calling it slate-gray, or perhaps ominous or inviting, and, before long, with luck, I'd also have located the beginnings of a mood. I'd be more interested in the mood. Or, attempting to name a mood, I'd name place—some Millville, say, of the mind. New Jersey itself was little more than incidental scaffolding.

"Use what's lying around the house," Mae West once counseled fellow raconteurs. It's also good advice for poets as long as "house" is defined broadly enough. Add to it imagination's furnishings, and it can seem you're paying extraordinary attention to what's around you. You include what's not readily apparent, find a language and a rhythm for it, and Voila!, it becomes part of what's there. That, ideally, is a poetry of place—some combination of the visible and the hard-to-see, that which the conventional eye can't apprehend until it's approached from a new angle and/or rearranged. Which is to say that poets create place as much as they depict it.

However, some twenty years ago, I must confess that not having paid much direct attention to place began to feel like a particular failure. I realized that almost all of my "landscapes" were inscapes, essentially psychological, and I attempted with some consciousness to remedy that. A long poem called "Loosestrife" was the immediate result, though in composing it I admit to being as interested in loose strife as I was in loosestrife, that rather insidious plant that takes over ecosystems. But I did employ the nouns appropriate to where I lived: marshland, red-wing blackbird, dwarf pine. It felt like an accomplishment. And then a few years later I wrote a whole sequence of poems called "Local Visitations." I placed 19th-century novelists in South Jersey towns, enabling me to see my environment through their rarefied sensibilities. Henry James was in Cape May. Dostoyevsky in Wildwood. Jane Austen in Egg Harbor City. So I suppose I'm on record now as someone who has attempted to invent where he lived.

Indeed, I use "invent" deliberately. In "Loosestrife," near the poem's end, I have a student ask why I'd stayed so long in South Jersey when I'd had many opportunities to go elsewhere. "Because it hasn't been invented yet," says the character who is the surrogate me. Maybe it's especially true of South Jersey, but it seems to me that all of New Jersey remains a literary opportunity. This is not to say that any particular poet should seize it.

Paradoxically, one of New Jersey's gifts to its poets is that it has freed us from such obligations. We have no historical wound to exert pressure on our imaginations, as there might be, say, in Virginia or Georgia. We have no idiosyncratic blend of Puritanism and individualism, as do states like Massachusetts and New Hampshire, no idiom peculiar to a collective ethos. Lacking a clear identity, New Jersey has allowed its poets to be *in* and *of* their environment yet at the same time liberated from any need of addressing some overarching sense of it. William Carlos Williams may have given us "Paterson" and snippets of local dialect from East Rutherford, but he was most interested in delivering to us an America. Truth be told, no poet worth his or her mettle wants to be defined solely by region, no less than by state. For the most part, we don't speak New Jersey; we speak from it.

With its multitudes, its smokestacks and rolling hills, New Jersey is as various as it is amorphous. So I'm glad that I have poems called "Beyond Hammonton," "Coming Home, Garden State Parkway," and "Atlantic City," glad that occasionally I've named how something felt in a particular place at a particular time, and, in the doing, registered what I think is New Jersey's most constant characteristic: its blend of the beautiful and the tawdry. But I'm also glad that most of my poems navigate in that somewhere between things as they seem and things as they are. That blur is what I try to be precise about. It has been my most urgent geography.

Mr. Flood's Party

"MR. FLOOD'S PARTY" is one of Edwin Arlington Robinson's Tilbury Town portraits, which, above all, show his mastery of tone and, in this case, how such mastery rescues—almost entirely—his subject matter from the bathos with which it flirts. "Almost" will be one of the concerns of this essay, though Eben Flood remains a memorable Robinson character, in the good company of Reuben Bright, Miniver Cheevy, Richard Cory, and the less defeated Cliff Klingenhagen.

Eben Flood, his aloneness intensified by old age, may or may not be a drunk, but on this particular evening he has the regular drinker's comic sense of self-imposed propriety. He needs to give himself permission. For some, it's when the sun is below the yardarm; for Eben, solitary that he is, it's the need for social drinking, for a companion, to have, as the title suggests, a party. It's one of the smallest and saddest parties ever registered in a poem, made so by Eben's elaborate formalities with his compliant alter ego. But the same formalities make us smile, too, which is Robinson's genius. We are regularly distracted from bathos by felicities both tonal and prosodic.

In rereading the poem, I found myself thinking of William Matthew's interesting preference for what he calls "aesthetic intimacy," which I take to mean a desire to work as closely as possible to one's subject while still orchestrating all of its effects. "Rueben Bright" and "Richard Cory" are also poems that display Robinson's gift for aesthetic intimacy, though their famous endings (one character tears down the slaughter house, the other goes home and puts a bullet through his head) succeed with tones so matter-of-fact that they suggest nothing if not what is commonly understood to be aesthetic distance. At the end of "Mr. Flood's Party," Robinson is working considerably closer to his subject. It may be why the last stanza doesn't resonate beyond what has already been established in the poem.

The poem's first stanza situates us immediately, both physically and psychologically. Its five-line opening sentence couldn't be better paced or orchestrated.

> Old Eben Flood, climbing alone one night
> Over the hill between the town below
> And the forsaken upland hermitage
> That held as much as he should ever know
> On earth again of home, paused warily.

Eben Flood is between a place that is forsaken and a town (we will soon learn) that no longer remembers him. And this hermitage of his "held as much as he should ever know / on earth again of home." The word that pricks us is "again" because it suggests that home was once a homier place and, no doubt, also because of its consonantal resonance with the plethora of other n-sounds, two of which are in "alone" and "forsaken." And how adroitly Robinson emphasizes "paused" after the long clause that establishes Eben's plight. The three iambs before it prepare us for an unstressed syllable. When, instead, we get a stressed syllable, we feel that a dramatic moment has been properly timed and delivered. Eben has paused, warily. He's about to begin his party, and it would be too embarrassing for him if others were about. In the lines that follow, we don't quite know how good and ironically understated "having leisure" is until we read further. And the road Eben's on is "his" in more ways than one, and more ways than one is how Robinson likes it.

"Well, Mr. Flood, we have the harvest moon / Again, and we may not have many more," commences Eben's address to himself and, almost in passing, allows us to hear that he doesn't expect to live much longer. The poet of "the bird is on the wing" that he refers to is Omar Khayyám. Eben has his prop; the social drinker offers a toast to the only companion he has, and acceptance is guaranteed. They drink to the bird in flight. It's a toast to the departed or the departing—an excuse to indulge, perhaps even a death wish. No doubt both.

The third stanza deepens what we already know, and the highly stressed "A valiant armor of scarred hopes outworn" distinguishes itself as language, while complicating our attitude toward Mr. Flood. (Eben is valiant; he no longer even has *scarred* hopes.) We learn that he once had been "honored" by his friends. The allusion to "Roland's ghost winding a silent horn" is either to Browning's "Childe Roland to the Dark Tower Came" or to the medieval French epic poem *La Chanson de Roland*. The former suggests a quest and the latter a kind of stubborn heroism. If it's the former, it's for purposes of comic disparity (Eben's quest is drink). If it's the latter, there's reason to receive it poignantly since the French Roland, trapped by the enemy, refused to blow his horn to signal help from Charlemagne's army until the moment of his death. Just as plausibly, it's there to suggest that Eben is like a ghost. He can hear the town's "phantom salutation of the dead" calling to him.

But in stanza four, his context firmly established now, Robinson most artfully makes his poem resonate beyond its sentimental concerns:

> He set the jug down slowly at his feet
> With trembling care, knowing that most things break;
> And only when assured that on firm earth
> It stood, as the uncertain lives of men
> Assuredly did not . . .

These are arguably the poem's finest moments, the poet allowing himself wise asides happily mitigated—though not reduced—by the fact that he's talking about a jug. No feel of the didactic here. These editorials on the human condition are rooted in setting and circumstance.

Eben's handling of the jug, which carries in it a temporary surcease of loneliness, is likened to the tenderness with which a mother would handle a sleeping child. This action is both comedic and heroic. We can imagine the slowness, the delicacy, with which a drunk puts something down so as not to break it. Eben is in the middle of a journey between two equally undesirable places, home and town; his heroism is in his effort toward good humor while he steels himself with drink. The jug is another character in the poem. In modern parlance, it's his baby, and he will care for it as such.

His invocation to his second self, his drinking companion, is more convivial at this point than self-pitying, though it's an edgy conviviality:

"... many a change has come / To both of us, I fear, since last it was / We had a drop together." The "I fear" registers with us, as does the end of his toast, "Welcome home!" We feel the irony in that last word, as Robinson wishes us to. It is, of course, emphasized by its placement and its rhyme. It should be noted that Robinson employs only two rhymes (with one exception) in each of his eight-line stanzas: at the ends of the second and fourth lines and the sixth and eighth. Here Robinson gets maximum effect out of rhyme, even though it's more near than exact. "Home" stops us, or is stopped for us by both its exclamation mark and the click of cooperative sound. We have not forgotten where he is. Home now is stupor, in the middle of nowhere.

The toast complete, Robinson successfully mimics the manners of the drunk who might also be a Puritan: "if you insist" and "Only a very little." This is an engaging burlesque within the larger, pathetic scene. Tonally, at this moment, we as readers are not asked to feel sorry for Eben. We are allowed to enjoy how well the poet, by blending tones, has been equal to the psychological and linguistic imperatives of his task. The lines that follow serve to further demonstrate Robinson's deft comic timing, which is linked to his metrical brilliance.

["]For auld lang syne. No more, sir; that will do."
So, for the time, apparently it did.
And Eben evidently thought so too;

Throughout, the poem has employed a mixture of blank verse and rhymed, often loose iambic pentameter. The iambic pentameter has been regular enough to permit Robinson many variations and substitutions. All the while, the illusion of natural speech has been maintained while "the grid of meter" has served as underpinning. The line "For auld lang syne. No more, sir; that will do" arguably has seven stresses. Only "For" and "No" and perhaps "will" would seem to be unstressed. But the prosodic fun occurs with the semicolon after "sir." It breaks the iamb-spondee-iamb flow of the line (a string of two-syllable feet), while conforming exactly to the way that we trust Eben's elaborate formality with himself would be spoken. The ten-syllable line has been kept but has been metrically fractured right at the point where Eben is telling his other self where to stop the pour. The narrative coyness inherent in "apparently" and "evidently" also serve the comic. Robinson would have us entertain that the narrator-observer, heretofore omniscient, is suddenly uncertain in this highly managed fiction. The uncertainty serves to underscore the narrative playfulness at this juncture, as does the placement of "did" after "do" as end words in successive lines. These are welcome balancing touches in a poem so potentially sentimental.

In the lines that follow, Robinson returns to a device that worked well for him earlier in the poem: the apparently positive word or phrase that in context suggests a harsh irony. Earlier, we were told "The road was his" and that Eben had "leisure." Now Eben is "secure," a word set apart by commas, which denotatively means he's not worried about being overheard singing out loud. We wait a full line before the "until" comes, and then his entire landscape echoes back to him the song of old times, which is his sad anthem.

I'm not sure what "with only two moons listening" is supposed to mean. It's a curious moment. My guess would be that Eben's selves each have a moon or, that to Eben's drunken eye, there appears to be two moons, but neither speculation satisfies. Frost's enigmatic reading of the two moons ("Two, as on the planet Mars.") in his "Introduction to Robinson's *King Jasper*" only seems to deepen the enigma.

When the landscape echoes "For auld lang syne," the poem reaches its climax. Eben cannot escape the sound of his own lamentation. Afterward, his "weary throat gave out" and the poem spirals into unrelieved pathos. It is in this stanza that Robinson's aesthetic intimacy—his ability to sympathetically deliver to us with multiple tones this sad and drunken man—fails him. He can only tell us more about how Eben feels. One longs for, if one is me, some resonance comparable to what he was able to effect in stanza four, a line that would evaluate and measure Eben's condition as much as it declares it. Some "slouching toward Bethlehem to be born" or, closer to Robinson's demonstrated gifts, his beautifully wrought last stanza of "Eros Turannos":

Meanwhile we do no harm; for they
    That with a god have striven,
Not hearing much of what we say,
    Take what the god has given;
Though like waves breaking it may be,
Or like a changed familiar tree,
Or like a stairway to the sea
    Where down the blind are driven.

The "we" is probably the townspeople and the "they" is a loveless couple in town who have somewhat tortuously stayed together. If only Eben, finally, were so perfectly enlarged and positioned for us. "Mr. Flood's Party" is a very good poem by a very good poet, as close to a great poet as a very good poet can be. Who knows, perhaps he's a great poet. I wouldn't argue. But in "Mr. Flood's Party," he wasn't able to pull back far enough to position Eben as sufferer as well as he was able to position the loveless couple. Aesthetic intimacy may, like most intimacy, be at its best when one keeps in reserve something peculiarly one's own to, at last, give away. Robinson, it seems, had said all he had to say about Eben halfway through the last stanza.

Learning How to Think

A Return to the Scenes of My Education

WHAT I'D LIKE TO TALK ABOUT TODAY are some of the ways Hofstra educated me, in and outside the classroom, and prepared me for navigating crooked paths, those paths we're likely to find ourselves on. A good liberal arts education can do just that: help us adapt to the uncertainties that lie ahead of us. In 1957, I was probably like most first generation college students—without reserves of culture or manners to draw from, somewhat of a stranger in a strange land. I had some athletic, but few academic models. I was serious-minded, but did not know how to translate that seriousness into good grades, or my habitual silence into something that might pass for contemplation. I imagine my teachers saw a quiet, attentive boy when they looked out into their classrooms. But attentive to what? (When I myself began teaching, some eleven years later, a fellow graduate student told me that at any moment you can count on the fact that sixty percent of your students are thinking of sex. This made teaching even more daunting than I had thought. How could I be as good?)

But I wasn't thinking of things from a teacher's perspective back then. I might have been thinking about sex, or basketball, perhaps even the fall of the Roman Empire. I was a history major, which meant I was accumulating valuable knowledge on my way toward unemployment. My guess is that if my teachers thought about me at all, they thought I was thinking of basketball. The college was small then. They probably knew that I was a pretty good player on a rather good team, and they chalked up my silence to a kind of goes-with-the-territory vacuity. And they might have been half-right. I could pivot and take a jump shot better than I could turn a phrase. But education occurs in various ways. I was learning some things that might help me when I came to certain crossroads. From literature, for example, that a doubt might serve a decision as well as a certainty. From history—at the risk of being equally reductive—that failure isn't necessarily defeat. I'll try to be more specific about these assertions as I go on. But perhaps by now you already feel in the presence of the kind of historian who has revised his past to fit his present identity.

Robert Frost's much misread poem "The Road Not Taken" comes to mind. It's a poem that flatters us into misreading it. Most of us can think of a juncture in our lives when we "took the one [road] less traveled by" and how "that has made all the difference." How we went to Hofstra, say, instead of Adelphi (though the roads to each were about equally worn), which is why we now own most of Nassau County, and are upright citizens, and have bright children and generous, smart, great-in-bed spouses. In the poem, Frost, in his sly way, is romanticizing his speaker's choice, and is allowing him to write his own press release in advance of any accomplishment. "I shall be telling this with a sigh / Somewhere ages and ages hence: / Two roads diverged in a wood, and I— / I took the one less traveled by, / And that has made all the difference." Well, if you read the poem carefully, the road chosen isn't the one less traveled by, and, besides, the verdict about the choice isn't in yet. The speaker is projecting (with a sigh, no less) that he made the right choice.

My talk faces a different danger. That somehow, against all odds, I've become a poet, that verdict is in, and I will therefore choose only those details that serve this version of myself. This exercise in retrospection will be fraught with omissions and slanted toward a construction of self that you should be wary of all the way through. Blame Hofstra. It can be argued that my intellectual life, such as it is, began in Dr. Judd's Historiography course in my junior year. History wasn't just history. It was told by people with their different persuasions and ways of seeing, often the victors, with different theories of history itself. A Marxist might describe a labor union strike differently than a free market capitalist. Of course! But how thrilling this was to the fledgling student. History was histories. For the sake of veracity, it always helped to know something about the teller. Stephen Dunn this evening will be trying to tell the truth about Stephen Dunn. You would be wise to consult other sources.

Let me start with basketball and the great Hofstra team I was part of, as well as coach Butch van Breda Kolff, and one of my teammates, Sam

Toperoff, and another, Richie Swartz. Because my subject today is education, I'll bypass the specifics of our accomplishments on the court, and concentrate on four things that have stayed with me just as importantly, if not more so: My introduction to what good talk is, an incident at Gettysburg College, a conversation overheard in a hotel room on another road trip, and the hidden rewards of disappointment. In other words, I will start with the kind of learning that occurred outside the classroom.

Good talk, I learned, was making keen and subtle distinctions about things you have observed, like, for instance—and I mean this seriously—When your opponent starts to dribble to his right, he always, after two dribbles, comes back to his left. Or he tends to always pull up for his jump shot after one dribble—observations that were as quietly thrilling to me as Kant's Categorical Imperative or Sartre's notion that existence precedes essence. Van Breda Kolff and his assistant coach Paul Lynner were philosophers of court sense and what to do and when to do it. They were masters of such talk. They made me aware of what an expert can bring to his subject.

Van Breda Kolff was a very bright, crude man, a Princeton graduate with a penchant for high spirits and vulgarity. He had played pro ball with the Knicks. A complicated man, he yelled a lot, happily farted in public, and one afternoon at the Gettysburg Hotel, when three of our African-American players were forbidden entry into the hotel game room, he immediately removed all of us from the hotel. This was 1960, Gettysburg of all places, the civil rights movement still in its relative infancy. Van Breda Kolff's intolerance for intolerance remains an early contribution to my moral education.

Sam Toperoff, who was to become a life-long friend, was a teammate, but six years older than I. He'd been in the army, as had been Dick Pulaski, another teammate, a philosophy major. Sam was the most interesting person I'd ever met, smart and iconoclastic, perhaps the most interesting undergraduate at the time at the college. (He eventually would be hired to teach at Hofstra, and author many books.) In his hotel room after a game (I can't remember where), he and Pulaski were talking about *Moby-Dick*, and I was there, not to participate, but to listen, which was my role, understood by all of us. It was the greatest conversation I'd ever heard. I had read the book, and loved it, and there they were articulating—the way good teachers do and good literature does—what I half-knew, but had no words for. Even more significantly, Sam was very funny. You could be funny about serious things! I'd not forget that. Sam would later become a large factor in my crooked-road drift to becoming a poet.

Around this time, I read *Crime and Punishment* and *The Brothers Karamazov*, the latter especially impinging on my life, or should I say my inner life, in ways that hooked me forever onto what great literature could do, dare I say the words, for the soul. That is, it made me realize I had one, and that it was underfed, in fact famished most of the time.

Then there was Richie Swartz, who replaced me as the starting guard on the Hofstra team that went 23 and 1. I had been one of the best players on the previous year's team when Richie was a freshman (freshmen couldn't play on the varsity team at that time). I played against him in practice, however, and if suffering has a positive side to it, as many say it does, I was learning on a daily basis something about humility, though perhaps humiliation is a more precise word. Richie Swartz, quite simply, was better than I was. It's entirely possible, had he not existed, and I had continued to be an important player on that Hofstra team, that I would have been at most a high school gym teacher (maybe even a successful one), instead of a poet and a college professor. Because of Richie Swartz I went further inward, found ways to live with disappointment. Thank you, Richie Swartz, you bastard.

Maybe it's time to read you a poem of mine about job hunting after college.

Everything Else in the World

Too young to take pleasure
from those privileged glimpses
we're sometimes given after failure,
or to see the hidden opportunity
in not getting what we want,
each day I subwayed into Manhattan
in my new, blue serge suit,

looking for work. College, I thought,
had whitened my collar, set me up,
but I'd majored in history.
What did I know about the world?

At interviews, if asked about the world,
I might have responded—citing Carlyle—
Great men make it go, I want to be one of those.
But they wanted someone entry-level,
pleased for a while to be small.

Others got the jobs;
no doubt, later in the day, the girls.
At Horn & Hardarts, for solace
at lunch time, I'd make a sandwich emerge
from its cell of pristine glass.
It took just a nickel and a dime.

Nickels and dimes could make
a middleman disappear, easy as that,
no big deal, a life or two
destroyed, others improved.
But I wasn't afraid of capitalism.
All I wanted was a job like a book
so good I'd be finishing it
for the rest of my life.

Had my education failed me?
I felt a hankering for the sublime,
its dangerous subversions
of the daily grind.
Oh I took a dull, well-paying job.
History major? the interviewer said, I think
you might be good at designing brochures.

I was. Which filled me with desire
for almost everything else in the world.

Well, I got that job. I had answered an ad in the *New York Times* for a writer (yes, I fancied myself something of a writer, which meant little more that I was pretty good at making sentences turn out grammatically), and I was hired by Nabisco to write in-house brochures and communiqués to the sales force. (This after turning down a job as a cub reporter for the *Flint* (Michigan) *Journal* because I realized I was too shy to ask strangers difficult questions about, say, some catastrophe that occurred in their lives.)

I was alarmingly good at that Nabisco job, and kept getting promoted, which terrified me. I wrote about Triscuits by day, and by night, for reasons of self-respect, tried to write fiction. I got married, found an apartment in Greenwich Village, continued to read voraciously and took courses at the New School in fiction writing and, later, poetry writing. On Sunday mornings, I played in a schoolyard basketball game on 10th Street that Sam Toperoff had invited me to, comprised of artists and writers. Sam's first novel had just been published, Calvin Trillin was already writing for *The New Yorker*, Christopher Lehmann-Haupt was reviewing books for the *Times*. Me, I had a good jump shot. Afterward, we'd all go back to Trillin's apartment where I remember Sam and Trillin brilliantly holding forth. More good talk. Again, no one expected me to speak. To my credit, I knew what interesting was. Therefore, I'd be quiet. I didn't know it then, but I was storing up.

The poetry writing course at the New School was taught by José Garcia Villa, a rather well-known poet at the time. I give Hofstra and in particular English Professor Chalfant credit for educating me enough so that I knew that almost everything Garcia Villa said was wrong. Or, if not wrong, not for me. I had begun to write poetry with some seriousness, and though I wasn't very good, I knew I didn't want to put a comma after every word (one of Garcia Villa's "experimental" tactics), or to always forsake sense for sound. As a result, I came to class prepared to argue, to find language for holding my ground.

I see it now as part of an effort—if you'll excuse the melodrama—to save my soul. Nabisco had just promoted me again, this time to a position that carried with it some prestige as well as money. I was 26. It's time to read you another poem.

The Last Hours

There's some innocence left,
and these are the last hours of an empty afternoon
at the office, and there's the clock
on the wall, and my friend Frank
in the adjacent cubicle selling himself
on the phone.
        I'm twenty-five, on the shaky
ladder up, my father's son, corporate,
clean-shaven, and I know only what I don't want,
which is almost everything I have.
        A meeting ends.
Men in serious suits, intelligent men
who've been thinking hard about marketing snacks,
move back now to their window offices, worried
or proud. The big boss, Horace,
had called them in to approve this, reject that—
the big boss, a first-name, how's-your-family
kind of assassin, who likes me.
        It's 1964.
The Sixties haven't begun yet. Cuba is a larger name
than Vietnam. The Soviets are behind
everything that could be wrong. Where I sit
it's exactly nineteen minutes to five. My phone rings.
Horace would like me to stop in
before I leave. *Stop in.* Code words,
leisurely words, that mean *now.*
        Would I be willing
to take on this? Would X's office, who by the way
is no longer with us, be satisfactory?
About money, will this be enough?
I smile, I say yes and yes and yes,
but—I don't know from what calm place
this comes—I'm translating
his beneficence into a lifetime, a life
of selling snacks, talking snack strategy,

thinking snack thoughts.
　　　　　　On the elevator down
it's a small knot, I'd like to say, of joy.
That's how I tell it now, here in the future,
the fear long gone.
By the time I reach the subway it's grown,
it's outsized, an attitude finally come round,
and I say it quietly to myself, *I quit,*
and keep saying it, knowing I will say it, sure
of nothing else but.

I did quit shortly after being promoted at age 26 to Advertising, Promotion, & Sales Relations Manager of a new Division, and set off to Spain to see if I could be a writer. It remains the most important decision I've ever made, and it couldn't have been done if I didn't have a supportive and adventuresome wife. Lois understood why I quit Nabisco and a very good salary, and did not worry that we were going to Spain, without prospects or contacts, with our meager savings of $2,200. I was going to write a novel, which I did, a very bad one, and I was going to save my soul, which I may have. The novel lacked certain ingredients, like plot and character, but it was full of inventive language. It helped show me that I should be writing poetry. We lived in Cádiz, Spain, for eleven months, until our money ran out.

In the meantime, Sam Toperoff, my only literary friend, my old Hofstra teammate, visited us with his wife, Faith. Their approval of the poems I showed them was crucial to me having a belief in myself. Faith had received her MFA in theater at the University of Iowa, and knew about the famous Iowa Writers' Workshop. I don't think I'd heard about graduate writing programs. I do know that without their urging I may never have applied to graduate school, and run into the great teachers that I had at Syracuse, or find myself moving in a direction that has allowed me to write what I have written.

I have been lucky. I have lived a writer's life, which of course can be a life without many rewards, and full of feelings of being neglected, not to mention envy, revenge, failure. I've had all those feelings, but also some rewards, and the pleasures of occasionally finding language for what cannot easily be said. To be a maker of poems is often to be a clarifier of mixed feelings, is to find yourself awash in ambiguity, and on the elusive edge of making some sense of the world. Who woulda thunk it possible, back in 1957 walking the quad toward Memorial Hall in my blue blazer, a few daunting, just-purchased books under my arm? Certainly not I, or anyone I knew at the time.

I want to conclude with the only basketball poem I've ever put in a book. You'll see it has to do with failure and diminishment, what in certain moods I would call the human comedy.

Losing Steps

1.

It's probably a Sunday morning
in a pickup game, and it's clear
you've begun to leave
fewer people behind.

Your fakes are as good as ever,
but when you move
you're like the Southern Pacific
the first time a car kept up with it,

your opponent at your hip,
with you all the way
to the rim. Five years earlier
he'd have been part of the air

that stayed behind you
in your ascendance.
On the sidelines they're saying,
He's lost a step.

2.

In a few more years
it's adult night in a gymnasium
streaked with the abrupt scuff marks
of high schoolers, and another step

leaves you like a wire
burned out in a radio.
You're playing defense,
someone jukes right, goes left,

and you're not fooled
but he's past you anyway,
dust in your eyes,
a few more points against you.

3.

Suddenly you're fifty;
if you know anything about steps
you're playing chess
with an old, complicated friend.

But you're walking to a schoolyard
where kids are playing full-court,
telling yourself
the value of experience, a worn down

basketball under your arm,
your legs hanging from your waist
like misplaced sloths in a country
known for its cheetahs and its sunsets.

I'm honored to have been chosen as alumnus of the year, and to have this opportunity to speak to you tonight, and grateful for the ways things began for me here some fifty-five years ago. Trust that I don't hold

Hofstra responsible for whatever bad poems I may have written, or any of the less than stellar things I may have done in my life, which, as you have deduced by now, I have omitted from this talk. History, after all, if the word is broken apart, reads as his story.

The Education of a Heart

EVEN WHEN WE'RE AT OUR WORST our hearts keep pumping, will try to keep us alive. If the heart seems not to discriminate, it's just saving its energy for the long road ahead. It's a worker in the field of the body, ignorant at first but educable, the way the poorly paid, the abused, have ways of saying enough is enough, perhaps by slowing down, or by issuing sudden jolts of discomfort. A hurt heart is a great student, always taking notes, remembering the when and the why. It reports to the brain. When the reportage becomes too severe, the brain sometimes denies, forgets, takes its information underground. It thinks it's being protective, but beginning with Freud and Adler and Jung, et al., we know that such repression is doing quiet harm. Like something trapped it wants out, and has a variety of unattractive means for subverting good intentions, and avenging wrongs.

The happy heart works in the same field. Its wages are love and affection. It is its own charity; what it gives tends to circle back to it, double its size. Those who haven't been loved cannot understand that its apparent poverty is a form of wealth. It has a gift for withstanding hardship. It never whines, but transcends, nurtures. Needless to say a happy heart is a rare thing. A purely happy heart belongs to a person without experience, who hasn't been educated in the classroom of temptation, or in the various crucibles of sorrow. Or it belongs to a person who has passed with grace and bravery all the hard tests that await us. In either case, I'm talking about people so saintly they are relegated to become the heroes of our past, and the terrible make-us-feel-bad dinner companions of the present.

I think the well-educated heart, if we are lucky, starts with our mothers. To the extent that my heart has now and then deserved a B+, and has occasionally risen from failure, I owe such achievements to my mother. That a loving mother prepares us for the often strange and foreign world of women is simply, in my case, a fact. She died young, at 59.

I can't remember how or what I felt at the time. She had a bad heart, which had incapacitated her for almost fifteen years. It was a heart good in every other respect, except perhaps that it tended to favor me, her first born, over my brother. I was twenty-nine, and had gotten used to her half-life, and the frailty of her once robust body. If she were to walk to the corner store, she'd be exhausted. My wonderful grandmother, her mother, did most of the work around the house. My father had died the year before of a heart attack—a heart, one could say, that suffered from various complications, but that's another story. My heart worked just fine, and was lacking. It hadn't yet been wrenched into discovering its capacities. That's also another story, involving different kinds of loss and growth, emanating from another kind of loving.

On the day of my mother's death (now almost fifty years ago), my brother still lived at home. I lived with my wife a few miles away. Here's the poem that speaks to that occasion:

That Saturday Without a Car

For Ellen Dunn (1910–1969)

Five miles to my mother's house,
a distance I'd never run.
"I *think* she's dead,"
my brother said, and hung up

as if with death
language should be mercifully approximate,
should keep the fact
that would forever be fact

at bay. I understood,
and as I ran wondered what words
I might say, and to whom.
I saw myself opening the door—

my brother, both of us, embarrassed
by the sudden intimacy we'd feel.
We had expected it,
but we'd expected it every year

for ten: her heart was the best
and worst of her. Every kindness
fought its way through damage,
her breasts disappeared

as if the heart itself, for comfort,
had sucked them in.
And I was running better
than I ever had. How different it was

from driving, the way I'd gone
to other deaths—
my body fighting it all off, my heart,
this adequate heart, getting me there.

What I remember, as the poem suggests, is that I knew I should be feeling something. I loved her. I did not have about her the often mixed feelings associated with those who have nurtured and constrained us. And yet I felt quite removed from any describable emotion. Though I'm not sure of this, I may have decided to cry was a way of offsetting the need to say how I was feeling. It would take years for me to understand that there's no proper response to death.

A few years later, I'd work on another poem about her. It was an attempt to understand what her legacy was to me. And to do that I needed to tell a story that required a certain delicacy if I were not to vulgarize the experience. I kept getting it slightly wrong. Eleven years after its inception, I think I got it right. (The poem, called "The Routine Things Around the House," appears on page 17.)

The getting it right had to do with discovering that her legacy had more to do with teaching me limits than it had to do with making me feel comfortable with women, though the latter was also true. When I came to that realization, the poem's ending, which had eluded me for so long, arrived in a matter of seconds.

My mother had been a physically beautiful woman, and my poem mythologizes her into a woman with extraordinary poise and tact. I've lived with the poem so long now that all I can say is, if it isn't wholly true, it has replaced what happened with what is now the truth. It certainly enacts an emotional truth, something that I seem to much better deal with on the page than in person. My heart's education is ongoing.

My mother gave me permission to go forward in the world. When I came home with all C's after my first semester at college (I, the first person in the family ever to go to college), she showed my grades to all her friends, saying things like, "He's so smart. Look, he passed everything." She allowed me to cultivate a feeling of security amidst the chaos of adolescence. Or, who knows, she gave me permission to be negatively capable, something that I wouldn't know was a positive until graduate school when Keats praised Shakespeare for being at home with doubts and uncertainties. Maybe, in fact, she prepared me for a life of revision. In other words, for trusting that over time feelings could be located.

I think that men who expect to be treated well by women generally are. The opposite is certainly true. Men who have had unloving mothers tend to find lovers who will perpetuate what they've come to understand as love. This, of course, goes both ways. Years ago, I listened to a call-in radio show that emanated from New York, in which the host psychologist (I can't remember her name) had a favorite and I still think brilliant response to women who'd call in, and say things like "He beats me, insults me, but I know he loves me and I love him." The psychologist would say, "That's not what love feels like." Further questioning revealed that such behavior was their only model for loving. This is no longer news, but it was to me then. And I feel privileged to have had a different model, even though it was essentially flawed too.

Which brings me to my father and maternal grandfather and men who love women. Chivalry, of course, is a form of patriarchy. I've always tried not to treat women as if they were damsels in distress, or couldn't open car doors for themselves, or would cause them to act as if they were not my equal. I say "tried" because I've failed as often as I've succeeded. I grew up in a house owned by my maternal grandparents. I've told this story before in poems and in essays, so I won't tell it in detail again. The nice way to put it is that my grandfather loved women so much that he wanted many of them. My father loved women so much that he chose to cover up my grandfather's dalliances because he thought knowledge of such would be unbearable for my mother and her mother. He went to his grave with the lie that he lost the family money at the race track. In fact, he had given it to my grandfather to help pay his mistress's hospital bills. Such is my legacy on the male side. A man who mostly got away with his secret life. And another who ruined his own life in order to protect women from the truth. A scalawag and a man of stupid nobility. In my long first marriage to a woman who deserved better, I was both. Each in his own way was loving, though the radio psychologist would have said, "That's not what love is, or should be."

If my father contributed positively to the education of my heart, it was in the years before his self-destructive lie. I had parents who were good to each other and good to me for the first fifteen years of my life. After that he drank at the Fleet Street Inn until I was sent to fetch him for dinner. He was treated as a wastrel and bore it in silence. As I wrote in a poem,

> Nights he'd come home drunk
> Mother would cook his food
> and there'd be silence.
> Thus, for years, I thought
> all arguments were silent
> and this is what I arm myself with
> and silence is what I hate.

And later in the same poem:

> I carry silence with me
> the way others carry snapshots
> of loved ones. I offer it
> and wait for a response.

I was burdened with knowing both sides of the story. It may be a virtue in poetry writing; otherwise it's a dilemma. I knew why my mother behaved as she did. I knew why my father didn't want to come home. My grandfather died, and never fessed up. My grandmother outlived all of them. She, I would learn years later, had secrets of her own. My heart learned from its own failures, and the failures of those I loved.

The education of a heart is never complete. As I write this, I worry about my omissions, my tendency to use words as a smokescreen. The heart is not a truth-teller; it wishes to say how it feels, which some people mistake for honesty. It can never be wholly trusted. It's always on the verge of being foolish. And mother love is always complicated by father love, and vice versa. The heart breaks, and is broken. That's part of its education. Sometimes it never heals. Sometimes it makes fabulous comebacks.

Carson McCullers said, "The heart is a lonely hunter." Lonely hunters are dangerous people, as are people who find reasons to justify hurting others. Albert Camus, a hero of mine, said, "I never said I was a good man, I only said that I try to be one." And William Meredith, in his wonderful poem written to Nixon during the Cambodian bombings, wrote,

A man's mistakes (if I may lecture you), his worst acts,
aren't out of character, as he'd like to think,
are not put on him by power or stress or too much to drink,

but simply a worse self he consents to be.

There are very few moral certainties that I admire. Meredith's is one of them, yet I tend to worry about statements that I can easily assent to. This one is part of a narrative strategy that indicts while demonstrating a trustworthy complicity. The narrator is like Camus; his self-knowledge has a complex modesty to it. Good judgment comes from experience, and experience, well, comes from poor judgment. In other parts of the poem, Meredith admits to sharing some of the bad judgment of which he's accusing Nixon. Nixon may have earned his nickname—Tricky Dick, and worse monikers than that—but as another poet, James Wright, reminds us, "the hearts of men are merciless." I would add, even the hearts that have been well-educated.

Words like *mostly, maybe, no, could have been*, sum up the education of my heart pretty accurately. I was a consenting adult who loved women easily and sometimes well. I mostly didn't throw the first stone. Maybe I could have been less indulgent, less selfish. No, I should have been. At important times I was silent when I should have explained myself. Most of my regrets are intertwined with my pleasures. At age 61, I found my true love. All the people in my past, especially my mother, participated, contributed, schooled my heart for such an occasion. I wouldn't have been ready for her without them.

Truth in Poetry

IN AN ESSAY OF HIS, Lawrence Raab, a poet with a fine, discerning mind, says that truth in poetry becomes an artistic concern, an act of transformation, or, as he deftly puts it, "a staged reenactment." I admire a great deal of what he says, but I think one can go a little further. Fernando Pessoa provocatively says, "The great artist should never have a really fundamental and sincere opinion about life. But that should give him the capacity to feel sincere, nay, to be absolutely sincere about anything for a certain length of time—the length of time, say, which is necessary for a poem to be conceived and written" (tr. by Edwin Honig). The implication here is that the poet is or should be a fictionist. We would have no trouble agreeing with this if we were thinking, say, of Shakespeare, but I'd like to discuss (eventually) a few contemporary poems that might add something to the question at hand.

The more personal or autobiographical the poem the more what should or should not be included in it becomes an issue for the author. Would any of us say that his mother was a whore (when she wasn't) because that detail helped make his poem work? I wouldn't, but I can imagine contexts where someone might. Or, if in fact she was a whore, for what purpose would you want your reader to know this? Well, perhaps the poem is exploring how you survived your childhood, or its tone is sympathetic, that what she did was a way of putting food on the table for her children. The awful details about Weldon Kees's daughter are redeemed because we learn they are part of an overall strategy. Raab says that "we feel manipulated but not betrayed," and "poems that correct themselves within themselves" produce a kind of literary pleasure." This is another way of saying that the poet has built into his poem the terms on how it should be read. If such a tactic were to fail, we might call the poem immoral or at least a contrivance, a word that has a similar but slightly more damning connotation than "manipulated" does. But all poems are contrivances we call art when they satisfy, or are good enough make us suspend our disbelief. Isn't truth in a poem, like honesty, always an achievement, a successful illusion?

The issue gets stickier when we are familiar, as we are in Lowell's case, with the author's biography. If there is such a thing as an author's covenant with his readers, as Raab suggests there is, how much fictive latitude should the reader give the author? I would say what Raab says, "the truth of a poem is the *poem's* truth," but to properly measure such truth often involves knowing the poet's track record. If we sensed, for example, that Lowell's fabrications served no other purpose that self-aggrandizement, or if what he made up constituted a form of self-indulgence, then that's when *author*ity breaks down. But if we sense that the choices he makes in "Skunk Hour," factually true or not, are in service of a larger purpose, some emotional veracity, and if that is the apparent case in many of his poems (which it is), then we're inclined not to worry about details that otherwise help complete the poem.

Shakespeare, especially in his plays, was able to inhabit the lives of his characters and seamlessly entertain their ideas and prejudices. He is Pessoa's model of the great artist demonstrating the capacity to be sincere for the duration of the work. But I want to talk about a few poems that don't raise the issue of being true in any factual sense, but nevertheless explore by absurdist or fantastical means different aspects of what can, for the duration of the poem, be believed. Let's look at this poem by Russell Edson, a poet who exclusively writes prose poems and begins nearly all of them with an absurd premise.

Rat Fever

A rat owns a man, which it operates with apron strings from its rathole in the wall.

The rat has the man to sit on a chair and to have his hands on his knees, and to sit there and to think, which for the largeness of the man's head he is supposed to do.

When the man's mother visits him he says he's a rat's thing.

Because the woman would tie the man to her apron and cause him to go away with her, the rat pulls the excuse me-string, and the man excuses himself for the bathroom.

Then the rat pulls the prepare-to-cut-string, and the man takes out his razor.

Then the rat pulls the cut-one's-throat-string, and the man cuts his own throat.

When the mother finally goes to see what keeps her son she finds him dead with his throat cut.

She sees apron strings coming out of one of his pant legs, and follows them back to a hole in the wall where a rat's eyes are beady, looking out at her.

She ties the strings to her apron and begins to dance. This drags the rat out by the fingers of its paws.

As she dances the rat is swung against the walls, until it is dead.

The blood of her son returns to his throat. His throat becomes uncut. He returns the razor to its place.

He says, I dreamed I was a rat's thing.

No, you are my thing, she says as she ties him to her apron.

It's a poem that readily admits to being a fiction, one that demands to be judged by a different sense of what constitutes truth. It is both funny and serious in the way the problems often are of dysfunctional families. Edson's task is to sustain his poem's imaginative logic, and in so doing throw a revealing light on a mother-son relationship. The poem, I'd argue, isn't "true" until we reach its conclusion. Prior to that moment, we're in the realm of fancy. We may be enjoying the poem's macabre narrative, even trusting, if we are familiar with other Edson poems, that it's on its way toward some kind of seriousness, but for a long while it runs the risk of just being inventively silly.

Formally, the poem has only itself to which to be true. The world that exists external to the poem consists of some broad awareness that this hyperbolic scene has a basis in reality. To falsify would be for Edson to violate the poem's eerily comic terms, to suddenly become too earnest or preachy. At any rate, we are not worried about a violation of personal disclosure. The mother is an emblem of a certain kind of mother. Maybe Raab's essay should be called "The Many Ways Poems Can Be True."

I won't quote James Dickey's "Sheep Child" in its entirety because it is fairly well-known. But it combines the realistic and the surreal, and in terms of this discussion posits whether good *what-if* poems are, or can be, as true as good *this-happened* poems. In the second half of the poem, after establishing in the first half that the speaker is aware that bestiality does occur among farm boys and sheep, Dickey has the sheep child, the product of such an act, speak the rest of the poem from its formaldehyde jar in an Atlanta museum. The poem asks *if* such a creature could speak, what would it say? The poem's ostensible weirdness is offset, I'd argue, by a non-moralistic sympathy with seeing "for a blazing moment / The great grassy world from both sides, / Man and beast in the round of their need…" If poetry, as many have stated, is an act of saying the unsayable, surely this poem qualifies as such an example.

Biography doesn't complicate Edson's poem. Most of us know nothing of his childhood, or even his adulthood. For Edson, we can posit that some aspect of the perverse is part of what it means to say the unsayable, not to mention to saying something true. For him such saying doesn't feel like a matter of courage the way it sometimes does with Dickey. Edson seems to be having a lot of fun with even his darkest inventions. Dickey's biography, like Lowell's, sometimes has to be taken into consideration when we attempt to assay the true. But aren't all poems innocent until proven faulty? If we believe them, aren't they true? And aren't experiential poems, well-made, just less obvious fictions than poems that overtly announce themselves as fictions? "A staged reenactment," Raab calls them. Artifice, or successful management of effects, is what has occurred in those poems that feel true. Untransformed events—a list of things that are included because they happened to us—are our failed poems. We haven't challenged them enough to discover something new. Our fidelities falsify.

Something Like the Truth

IT WAS ALMOST OCTOBER and several months earlier I had agreed to do two things: give a lecture at Stockton College (where for a long time I'd taught) to a 9/11 course being taught by friends of mine, and one as well at West Virginia University as part of my Jackson Professorship obligations. Obligations? I mean pleasures, of course. The course at Stockton had become such an event that, in order to house the many people who enrolled in it, it had to be held in the Performing Arts Center. My friends had asked several scholars and journalists to give guest lectures, and they asked me if I would address the issue of "The Artist after 9/11" or "The Poet After 9/11." I thought, well, I can do that, after all I'm a poet and have many thoughts and feelings about that terrible day and the days and months that followed.

But every time I sat down to write that talk I would say something for about two paragraphs that I believed to be true, and then realize I either didn't believe it, or could entertain so many competing thoughts that the prospect of continuing seemed daunting, almost impossible. I'd put it aside, write a poem instead, or play tennis, or watch television, that box that brought into my house the awful world, seemingly getting awfuller by the moment. And then a few weeks later I'd start again, have another false start, or come smack up against my ignorance of some necessary historical scaffolding, decide I was too lazy to do the research, and go instead to the movies, anything to get away from writing this talk.

For example, I wanted to take on what seemed, in practice, worrisome about some of Islam's followers, but I didn't know enough about its strengths in order to take it on intelligently. What I really wanted was to excoriate fundamentalists, not just Islamic fundamentalists, but all kinds, but then that seemed too easy to do, and I hardly would be bringing the news to anyone. I wanted to say that for years I've known that fundamentalists were my enemies, that it might be better for someone to have read no books at all than to have read one and believed everything in it. I was thinking of the Bible as much as I was the Koran. One-book folks, of course, tend to be frighteningly intolerant, enemies at the very least of ambiguity and ambivalence, two of my dearest words, not to mention conditions.

But then I'd think history is full of people like Pound whose breadth of reading didn't keep him from being politically and morally foolish, and terrible others like Göring who had a keen appreciation of art. And we know that Saddam Hussein wrote a novel and Mao Tse-tung was a poet, for Christ's sake, who eliminated thousands of his countrymen and forged that epitome of mindlessness, the Cultural Revolution. So how to figure? Which was why I abandoned that line of thinking, and thought of writing an essay I'd long contemplated, "The Dishonesty in Honesty," wondering if in the process I could make it touch on concerns pertinent to 9/11. Wondering, too, if I could make my case without succumbing to some of honesty's apparently attractive, but dubious qualities. A heartfeltness, say, or any of its various forms of do-gooderness, so often in league with the righteous.

I would need to remember Faulkner's Nobel speech, and his insistence that great literature comes "from the human heart in conflict with itself." One implication of that statement is that for honesty to be honest it might need to acknowledge contradiction, or at least the difficulty of reconciling or living with opposites. Another implication is that it might take a great fictionist to even approach something like honesty, that its varieties and permutations might be better understood if they were dramatized rather than asserted.

I had long mistrusted people who professed honesty without any traces of self-doubt, and I worried that in these post-9/11 days so many people suddenly seemed so earnest and righteous, so without doubt about right and wrong, about the good guys and bad guys, and we had a President with a vocabulary that matched such reductionist simplicities. He was sure that evil resided in three places, count 'em—and on an axis of all things. The unimaginative and the non-introspective seemed particularly inclined to speak the language of honesty, and in bin Laden or Bush we had two rather out-front, shoot-from-the-hip cats. Each had little interest in the difficulties in making forays toward the true, that higher form of honesty. With bin Laden truth was something religious and received. With Bush it was always a little slow to arrive. If and when it did, we trusted that his advisors would have to point it out to him. But to write that talk/essay I'd have to explore—if I wanted to be truthful about the dishonesty in honesty—my own complicity in regard to it, my considerable history of using the language of honesty with my poker face while I was concealing or meaning something else—and I wasn't sure I was ready yet to take that on. "The pleasures of ulteriority," Frost called such tactics, but he of course was speaking about poetry in which fabrications are often virtues. In personal relations, a different matter entirely. If I were to take it on, I certainly would need to be mindful of what Stephen L. Carter wrote: "Honesty is most laudable when we risk harm to ourselves; it becomes a good deal less so if we instead risk harm to others when there is no gain to anyone other than ourselves."

Yes, I had better save "The Dishonesty in Honesty" for another time. The facts, I decided, would have to do for a while. I'd begin with them, knowing how tinged with feelings they would need to be if they were to matter at all. Emotional fact—the territory of poets. Like many on 9/11, I sat before the TV watching the reenactments of the planes crashing into the Trade Center, alternately weeping and benumbed, believing my whole world had changed, and wanting vengeance, yes, let's get the fuckers, I thought. I felt violated, and played over and over in my mind what must have been the horror of the victims' last moments. Everyone did, I'm sure. It took no special powers of the poet to imagine such moments. But it would take skill to frame and position them. In many respects, the events of that day overwhelmed our abilities, as artists, to deal with them. It certainly overwhelmed mine. It was a time to point the unemotional camera and click.

For a while photography was king. At its best, it gave us more than we had seen, usually what poetry also offers. But for me, to speak then was to mumble, choke up. The inclination to watch far exceeded any inclination to write. Later, the poets might and would deliver the murky interiors of that experience. But not then. The New Yorker had a photograph that no poem at the moment could equal: a man covered with white dust, sitting amid rubble with his laptop; you couldn't tell if he was a statue or an actual man, or if an actual man whether he was dead or alive.

It took many weeks for me to realize I had become as single-minded as any fundamentalist; I'd lost whatever complicated sense of politics I'd had, lost as well my poet's ability to enter the mind of the other. I had become a simple patriot with a patriot's characteristic blindness. I even admired the President's firm resolve. But I started to feel soulless, uncomfortably aligned with power and its rhetoric. My daughter and her husband, each humanely political, were immediately concerned about an excessive American military response that would result in countless deaths beyond those of the Taliban and al-Qaeda. Though their pacifism seemed to me insufficiently thought out, their worries about my hawkishness helped restore in me some of my old deliberative faculties. "Perhaps," I heard myself saying again. And "On the other hand..." And "What if..."

So once more I thought I could fashion a new talk. I'd write about how I recovered some of my old vocabulary, and with it some historical perspective, a geopolitical overview. I'd rail about the ubiquitous "God bless Americas" coming from the same voices that were attacking the religious fanaticism of the terrorists. Imagine thinking, I'd begin, that if there were a God he'd be on our side! I'd have a little theological fun. But then of course again I'd think about how my country and its people had earned their outrage and grief. That we had been viciously attacked, that no one's broader politics should diminish that fact, or prevent one from lamenting the carnage, and that there were real enemies out there with plans to kill us, and that "us" included me. So I'd stop again, all the while aware I'd promised Paul and Dave, those politically and socially conscious good friends, this talk. Both of them were capable not only of thoughtfulness, but activism as well. I envied them that. Not only was I a slacker when it came to writing a talk, I realized that if I could write it, that's all I would do. I was somewhat famous at the college for behind the scenes thinking, almost no record since the Vietnam war of overt action. I began to feel unworthy of the task.

Wasn't this a time to become a public man? Plus I was hiding something, something post-9/11 that was perhaps closer to my own fraught truth than any lingering memory of buildings imploding or dogs sniffing for life. One week after the attacks I'd left my long marriage, shocking my wife and others, and, most of all, myself. I'd fallen in love with someone else, becoming a love-terrorist to some, a brave man to others. Depending on one's perspective, I might have been the South Jersey equivalent of one of those plane-crashers: the man who did something destructive for what he believed was a higher good. I admit that for me the reality of living with what I'd done, the large pleasures and sadnesses that devolved from it, superseded all the national news.

Could I write about that? Would it be a gratuitous, self-serving honesty or would it serve some truth? Certainly to leave it out of my talk, by implication, would be to tell someone else's truth, not mine. I was back to thinking about my discarded subject, "The Dishonesty in Honesty." And here I was doing what I said I wasn't ready to do, speaking "honestly" about events in my life in which I had left a trail of lies. Straight-faced lies that had given me certain latitudes, that facilitated a divided heart.

Sissela Bok defines a lie as "any intentionally deceptive message which is *stated*." Such a definition does not include our lies of omission, which also tend to give us a temporary advantage over those to whom instead we give only our well-timed silence. About one month after 9/11 I wrote a poem, a villanelle, that on its surface evokes the kind of deception the hijackers must have pulled off in order to be successful. One of its refrain lines is "Easy for anything to occur." But I doubt the poem would have turned out the way it did had I not been thinking as well about my own situation.

Grudges

Easy for almost anything to occur.
Even if we've scraped the sky, we can be rubble.
For years those men felt one way, acted another.

Ground Zero, is it possible to get lower?
Now we had a new definition of the personal,
knew almost anything could occur.

It just takes a little training to blur
a motive, lie low while planning the terrible,
get good at acting one way, feeling another.

Yet who among us doesn't harbor
a grudge or secret? So much isn't erasable;
it follows that almost anything can occur,

like men ascending into the democracy of air
without intending to land, the useful veil
of having said one thing, meaning another.

Before you know it something's over.
Suddenly someone's missing at the table.
It's easy (I know it) for anything to occur
when men feel one way, act another.

This poet, then, after 9/11? Tortured, but not for just the obvious reasons. "Nothing would be the same from here on," that omnipresent refrain, now for me would forever mean at least two things. Yet couldn't I imagine that for most North Americans the aftermath of 9/11 was also experienced through a double lens, the inevitable exigencies of their normal lives gradually taking hold? And for most middle-class North Americans, regardless of their perfidies and hardships, that meant a quality of life better than 90% of the people in the world. Even if your marriage had just broken up, you weren't a Bosnian or a Rwandan or, for that matter, a Palestinian. I was drifting again.

Should I, I thought, write about that? Try to write an apologia for terrorists? Attempt to assay the lies that serve a cause, and the honesties that wouldn't? Should I remind my audience that our one tragic day, to one bad degree or another, is endured day after day in countries throughout the world? I have to get this thing written, I'd say to myself each time. But so many thoughts lived with other thoughts that I couldn't sustain a paragraph, no less a 45-minute talk. Maybe one way to tell something like the truth, I decided, is to ramble, to offer the simultaneities of a jumbled mind about what poet Robert Hass calls our "navigable sorrows," the things we endure and survive.

At this juncture of history, could I say out loud and without embarrassment that I've never been happier? That also I've never felt a loss so deeply? Is it obscene to be happy in such a vicious and disgraceful world? Is it obscene to think my self-brought-about sadness matters in such a world? Should I worry about the reaction of anyone who doesn't love contradictions? Or paradox? Can we admit that 9/11, that shorthand for carnage, has become (circa October 2002) a kind of deadened slogan, that the more we say it the less awful it becomes? Every time I sat down to write this talk, I was aware that I'd be speaking it to students who by then would have been overloaded with information and opinions about the subject no doubt more informed than mine. And who probably would have heard the term 9/11 so much that it would have the ring of a convenience store they might shop in, or a soft drink they might buy there. And should I tell them I was sure that in the future, if not already, there'd be 9/11 jokes, perhaps even a rock band with that would vulgarize its tragedy.

Who could have thought in 1963 or 1968 that there ever could be a band called The Dead Kennedys? Maybe, thought I, I should scrap this ramble entirely, speak instead of something I actually know about—the difficulties of writing a good political poem. But wouldn't that bore them to tears? Or worse, that I would devalue the necessary speech of poets who wrote 9/11 poems just because what we/they wrote wouldn't hold up to time's wiser judgments? Would it be fair to compare my poem "Grudges" and their poems to, say, "Easter, 1916" or Paul Celan's "Death Fugue"?

Let time be the wise guy, I decided. Let me praise the need to give voice to that which is difficult to say. Maybe, to risk more unflattering comparisons with greatness, I'd incorporate the poem I wrote to a terrorist in 1988, a poem that arose out of the need to find language for my impotence and ineffectuality in the face of atrocities, like Lockerbie. Yes, I thought, I'd mention Yeats and Celan, then offer Dunn. Why not, I've taken every other liberty with this piece. Here goes. It's called "To a Terrorist," and in fact I will not apologize for it. Perhaps it will contribute a little to partially conveying something like the truth.

To a Terrorist

For the historical ache, the ache passed down
which finds its circumstances and becomes
the present ache, I offer the poem

without hope, knowing there's nothing,
not even revenge, which alleviates
a life like yours. I offer it as one

might offer his father's ashes
to the wind, a gesture
when there's nothing else to do.

Still, I must say to you:
I hate your good reasons.
I hate the hatefulness that makes you fall

in love with death, your own included.
Perhaps you're hating me now,
I who own my own house

and live in a country so muscular,
so smug, it thinks its terror is meant
only to mean well, and to protect.

Christ turned his singular cheek,
one man's holiness another's absurdity.
Like you, the rest of us obey the sting,

the surge. I'm just speaking out loud
to cancel my silence. Consider it an old impulse,
doomed to become mere words.

The first poet probably spoke to thunder
and, for a while, believed
thunder had an ear and a choice.

From the beginning of time, or at least from the beginning of language, poets felt the need to address what they feared, what was just beyond their ken, even to proffer unpopular truths. At the outset, they did it for the commonality of the tribe, but now so few of us belong to a tribe with shared values and beliefs, we do it first for ourselves, hoping to be overheard by the few others who might care and listen. 9/11 aside, that's the American poet's lot, to continue to speak into the void because we have to, because we're habituated to respond to what's in front of us, even if it's nothingness, the wilderness cry that, at best, years later, might become part of the culture. My terrorist poem is one of sympathy and contempt, the two intermingling. Acts of terror? To the cool historical eye, no doubt acts of terror are matters of relativity. Everyone has a good reason. We assassinated Allende in Chile, paving the way for that monster Pinochet, because we were protecting ourselves from communism, or so we thought. We supported the Shah in Iran, and then wondered why so many Iranians were out to get us. As is often pointed out, the difference between a suicide bomber and a freedom fighter is a matter of who gets to write history.

What's the role of the artist after 9/11? I wouldn't proscribe it. We know reality exerts pressure on the imagination to respond to it. This, for the artist, will always be the case. But it's also true that most artists are contrarians, and will go their own way. Post-9/11, we're just as likely to get poems about butterflies as we are about bombs. And some of those insufferable postmodernists will not be moved to make sense any more than they ever were, though it was tempting for a while to think they'd be shamed into writing about the recognizable world. And occasionally we're going to get poems that walk the line between good and bad taste, often my favorite kind. Recently, an interesting graduate student poet of mine began a poem with, "Sometimes a hug is more dangerous than a blow job." A few of us in class even knew what he meant, were grateful for the insight. Some laughed. I was quite pleased that no one seemed to disapprove. It struck me that his poem had something to do with freedom, a freedom that wouldn't exist in bin Laden's world. In pursuit of my elusive essay/talk, I realized, such drift and counter-drift was emblematic of how my mind worked; I'd never get it written. Unless of course that was its form. Aha! And now here I am, well on my way to completing a talk about the various talks I could have almost given this evening. Postmodern of me, no? With his opening line, my student probably wanted to shock us into attention. But then he had the serious and hard task of sustaining such provocativeness, of getting out of the poem successfully, which he did. His last line was, "If you meet yourself on a road, shoot first." It was a play off of the Buddhist wisdom, "If you meet the Buddha on a road, kill him," the essence of which is that each of us has to find his or her own truth, we can't rely on anyone else's.

I don't know if I'm going to get out of this provocatively or success-fully, but I will say that in general I'm suspicious of honesty because it often gets in the way of the truth, much as religion gets in the way of the spiritual. In politics, where truth is often irrelevant, it sometimes just gets in the way of effectiveness. I feel comfortable in poker games because I know that everyone in the game understands that everyone else is trying to deceive them. In a sense it's the most "honest" of games. Power is a blend of how good your cards are, how well you're able to play them, and your ability to read your opponents. By necessity, there's a kind of perpetual détente among good players. It does no good to bully. The player who puts his pistol on the table, and then raises, might win that one hand. But he sets in motion the end of the game, or, worse, players packing guns the next time.

The dynamic is not unlike what occurs in international politics. We expect from leaders of countries nothing less than a craftiness which will help insure the furtherance of their nation's best interests. In that respect, à la Machiavelli, we don't expect statesmen to be honest, only to appear hon-est. Machiavelli says that "Rulers must free themselves from the authority of virtue in order to feign it." Bush's problem is that he actually believes that he and the United States are virtuous. He hasn't freed himself from virtue, and therefore can't use it as a tactic. Nor is he able to successfully imagine how he is perceived by other nations and their leaders.

He's on the verge, if he goes through with this war on Iraq, of be-coming as dangerous as bin Laden, who also equates everything he does with virtue. Bush has got the gun at the table, and he's going to use it because he thinks the other guy has a hidden gun, though he's not sure if it's loaded. He may even be right; time will tell. But when in doubt exercise power, is bad poker playing in the long run. One, if one is me, can only be happy that international resistance and Ramadan and other circumstantial pressures have caused him, of late, to be prudent. Power combined with righteousness is a scary thing. In this case, it's sure to spawn a dialectic that will do us no good.

Whatever the outcome, poetry will respond to it, though I can't imagine that will result in any solace, which was something, by the way, the populace sought from poetry after 9/11. Fine. But I'd like the American public to look to poets and poetry for criticism too, for subversion of what passes for the truth. And poetry will continue to find new ways to talk about roses and limn the varieties of love as well. A little over one year has passed since 9/11 and since I left my marriage. I feel and think many contradictory things. I do not and cannot represent the artist after 9/11. Or anybody, really, except myself. My life has radically changed, and I'm the same person I always was, a man of numerous identities, and a moral struggler whose actions can't bear much scrutiny, but a struggler nonetheless.

If I met myself on a road, a post-9/11 road, I think I'd try to walk with me for a while, maybe shoot me later. I don't know. I confess, though, and you should be aware that one is rarely honest when he confesses, that post-9/11 and post-breakup and advent of new love, I shun those righteous ones who seem never to have happily held two opposing thoughts or loved two women at the same time, or can't imagine doing so.

I have my poet's mind back, for better or worse. At best it's capable of—in Auden's terms—the clear expression of mixed feelings, though this talk probably suggests that it hasn't been quite at its best. It's saying to me now, Get al-Qaeda, sure. Get Hussein, maybe. But let us question ourselves about starting invidious wars and killing lots of people. The discerning leader, the person who has earned his honesty, who has put his beliefs to hard tests, tends to hesitate, measure, refine. You can hear those qualities in his voice, which must, ideally, be a passionate voice too. We need him now, and he's nowhere in sight.

The one-dimensional thinker speaks without commas, without clauses. Bush served his purpose immediately after the Trade Center/Pentagon attack. He was doubtless and firm, the same qualities that are scary in him now. But then I think—and no doubt by now you know that if intelligent ambivalence is one of my virtues, it's also one of my problems—that, yes, the heart in conflict with itself may indeed help produce great literature, but also can be an impediment to action. In dire circumstances it might give us a Chamberlain instead of a Churchill. But Churchill, we must remember, was responding to a clear and present danger, and was blessed with a silver tongue.

2002

One Summer

Musings about Avoidance, Temperament,
and the Poem Becoming a Poem

THERE'S SOMETHING TO BE SAID FOR AVOIDANCE, other than its obvious virtue—not doing what you're supposed to do. Last summer, for example, I planned to write a memoir about my grandmother's secret, which I had only recently learned, and instead made phone calls, lingered with my coffee, or found myself writing something else. One morning, turning away from my notes, I wrote this line: "Night without you, and the dog barking at the silence . . ." Next morning, "Maybe genius is its own nourishment, I wouldn't know." Both lines led to poems, one a love poem, the other about Glenn Gould, neither of which had anything to do with my grandmother. Apparently I had tapped into some rich vein of psychic refusal, a source of energy that seemed transferable to subjects not related to it. Of course I needed to believe that I actually wanted to write the memoir. When it was clear after a while that I didn't, my avoidance-as-compositional-method lost power. But I was able to fool myself for several weeks. I wrote more poems that summer, many of them keepers, than I had during any comparable time. It should come as no surprise that "What if" and "Let's see where this goes" were far more seminal than "Here's what happened."

"Avoidance" suggests psychological fear, something unresolved that tempts us while declaring Stay Away. I was avoiding something, but so what? As Fitzgerald has Gatsby say about Daisy's marriage to Tom, "it was only personal"—a strange disconnect that nevertheless freed him to pursue the wildness of his dream. Such suppression of reality would come back to haunt Gatsby, but that's another matter entirely. At the time, it gave him permission to go forward. Whatever my reason for resisting grandmother's secret, it kept leading me elsewhere, if not forward. And, that particular summer, elsewhere was where the unexpected, the loose-ended, the half-known, resided. Avoidance led me into unforeseen areas, which is only to confirm that poems originate in unlikely ways. Then it helps that you've devoted your life to developing and honing the skills that might take you further. Like opium or free writing, avoidance may get you into a poem, but rarely out of one.

After all, it takes a lot of things-in-place just to become a merely decent poet. For starters, a passion for and a suspicion of language. Empathy for otherness. Contempt for sham, comfort with artifice. Some balance between truth's cruelty and irony's armor. A love of both exactitude and ambiguity. If we're not beginning poets, all of these qualities should be ingrained in us before the poem begins. They must remain the poem's informants—behind the poem, not in it, unconsciously guiding its decisions. Something galvanizes them if we're lucky. That something could be anything—"a wild horse taking a roll," as Marianne Moore says, or an uprising in 1916, or something utterly serendipitous, like the way language in the act of finding companionable language also finds meaning.

Of course, I don't think of any such things when I compose. And I try to forget about my heroes and their daunting qualities. Jeffers' ferocity. The artful delicacy with which Larkin distills and orchestrates his bile. Dickinson's quirky incisiveness. Dante's perfectly imagined hell. Shakespeare's capaciousness. Heroes can become hindrances. They, too, need to be unconscious, informing elements—assimilated, ingrained, part of who you are.

Avoidance, indeed. Some things need to be forgotten in order to proceed. One summer I couldn't shake "That is no country for old men," kept hearing it in my head every time I sat down to write. Yeats was too much with me. I took a lot of naps.

Some therapists, for our own good, might want us to confront what we tend to suppress. When I'm writing, I'm happy to be the healing profession's adversary. It may be true that our lives are more important than our poems, but not when we're working on one. Besides, no poet wants to end up with a poem that is the equivalent of learning how to cope. Poems need to be better than acceptable, better, certainly, than their authors. In the broadest sense, they should offer the reader a good time, which, by my lights, can include a sadness, or even the horrific, wonderfully enacted. I never understand when people say that a good poem about a depressing matter depressed them. I'm a sucker for the world as it is brought home anew, whatever it takes to deliver it. Paul Celan's "Death Fugue" elates me. Restraint, avoidance's mentally healthy cousin, has, in many quarters, a good reputation. I have been one of its practitioners. But there must be something large that enlists our restraint, else it be like building a corral for a mouse. I will grant restraint its virtues without listing them. We, the congenitally restrained, though, can't be too proud of ourselves for being so. Wouldn't we rather be praised for what's lesser in our natures—those times we've been excessive or expansive? Don't we love to reach that moment in a poem that makes us feel like we've just gotten back home, safely, with stolen goods, all traces of how we got there hidden? Aren't we most pleased when our restraint serves some wildness?

Stevens said some poets prefer a hard rain in Hartford to a drizzle in Venice, and vice versa. He wasn't elevating one over the other. He meant that, in varying degrees, we're all unconscious servants of our temperaments. Perhaps, but within a temperament I have to believe there's room for a good deal of variety. I like rock music, for example, but not heavy metal. I love Hopkins's passionate syntax, but I come to it with George Herbert's metabolism. I'd like to own one of de Kooning's Woman paintings and also Vermeer's *Girl with a Pearl Earring*. I suppose that my temperament inclines me to spend a longer time in front of the Vermeer; I love how quietly it invites contemplation. But the first time I saw one of the de Koonings my response was entirely and excitingly visceral. It disturbed, shocked. Now I find myself smiling in its presence. Like a disastrous love affair thought about years later, it has become comic. I've found another way to live with it.

I suspect that I'm a drizzle person with a hankering for a good storm, quick to put up his umbrella. But would I prefer the drizzle if it were in Hartford? In the Bronx? Isn't context ready to confound almost anything we feel sure of?

I've always been tempted to be what I'm not, first out of a sense that I wasn't much of anything, then out of a conviction that it was possible to create oneself. I can think of a few achievements I never achieved, lies I eventually turned into facts out of sheer embarrassment of being caught. (Don't ask me to cite them.) I can also think of those times I got caught. Certainly, though, as writers, we can expand who we are by entertaining or impersonating who we're not. Witness any persona poem, all those women reinventing Penelope to reinvent themselves, all those contemporized Oedipuses discovering how to see in the dark. And to write *is* to reach into the dark. Occasionally we touch something we didn't know we sought. Sometimes we get bitten, or worse. Sometimes there's nothing. We move forward, our imaginations as feelers. We make things up to find what is or isn't there.

Poetry writing is more humane than life! It's full of second chances. Your sentence, so to speak, can always be revised! You can fix the inappropriate, adjust every carelessness, improve what you felt. How perfect for someone like me: Unabashed avoidance one afternoon, a little excess in the evening, a few corrections in the morning. The various ways I've embarrassed myself, crumpled up, in the wastebasket, never to be seen.

But wait, there is of course the final product. If you're ambitious for your work, there is no hiding. It's not that I've revealed aspects of my life (though I may have) that's at issue. It's my skill and sensibility, which, combined, constitute style. And nothing is as personal or as individuating as style. My final product must be evidence that I've switched my allegiance from content to handling of content, that whatever intensity I've mustered has become increasingly aesthetic. Or, rather, there should be no evidence of this, just the poem standing for itself, tinged with the residue of a style, hopefully in some way distinguishing, if not distinctive.

For the record, the grandmother memoir finally got written, late that summer, as a poem. Much of what I've been musing about here went into the writing of it. In order to get started, I needed to veer into it, take it and myself by surprise. I'll not go through the many drafts of this poem, the many tinkerings and rearrangements, except to say I'd been thinking about the Buddhist saying, "If you meet the Buddha on the road, kill him," and began with it, then discovered that it needed to be withheld until later. Buddhism, in fact, would play a minor role in the poem, yet it was the beginning of some narrative latitudes not available to me had I stayed strictly with my subject. Purposefulness, that enemy of invention, suddenly had a harder time getting its way. I was free to let one perception lead to another perception, the facts of the matter now merely the cargo, not the engine. What was at stake were ways to be true to my poem while being true to grandmother's secret, and I confess my allegiance quickly tipped to the poem, as I've indicated it should, because only attention to the poem *qua* poem makes its contents significant. (The poem appears at the end of this essay.)

Writing poetry is about giving yourself permission for what you've found yourself to be doing. It follows, therefore, that it's an act both promiscuous and self-regulating, and that's how I like it. (Perhaps my avoidance of the memoir form was that it wasn't promiscuous enough.) My first wife used to say I wanted two of everything. It was a conservative estimate. But what I wanted and what I ended up doing were often vastly different, as they are in poems themselves—matters of compromise and adjustment. Of course I want to be who I am *and* many things I'm not. Drizzle man wants to be thunder man, and thunder man wants to conceal the lightning that caused him. My wishes, however, may not matter.

By early September, I'd reverted once again to the exigencies of my temperament. I remembered the pleasures of light rain and muted colors. The lure of subtlety. A measured response. Auden, Frost, Williams, Donald Justice—my mentors, unbidden, were tapping me on the shoulder. And, as ever, there was Apollo insisting I clean up after the fabulous party that had spilled into the street. Might as well dance a Danse Russe whenever I can, I concluded, might as well bend a few birches.

The Telling of Grandmother's Secret

> "Belle's story was that she came over from
> Prince Edward Island to Boston when she was
> sixteen to be a nurse's apprentice, but that
> wasn't exactly true. She got pregnant, had
> the child—oh it's a long story. The truth is
> she was sent away in shame."
> —Aunt Jessica, age 87

Trying to desire nothing,
I walked up Gravel Hill Drive,
then back, the day after Jessica's call.

But my disquiet wouldn't be quieted.
I was clear proof that unless you sat
very still, did the necessary work,
Zen was just a name, a kind of flirtation.

　　Still, nice to know there was a religion you could fail
without worrying about eternal damnation,
a conundrum troubling you instead of a precept.

　　Nice also to ramble toward your subject,
sensing nobody cares about it but you,
feeling those first narrative latitudes,
the narrowings as you go. Already the secret
had visited my sleep, sat down with me
at breakfast, rubbing the dark from its eyes.
What confidence it had. Imagine,
this suddenly unlocked thing
believing it was irresistible as is.

　　"I'm the only one left who knows,"
Jessica explained, then couldn't stop herself.
With each call the secret grew larger,
and I'd carry it out into the vagaries
of late October—one morning a clear view
of Savage Mountain, the next a cold mist—
aware that every story needed atmosphere
in order to exist.

　　And then the surprise of atmosphere
in collusion with memory, grandmother's silence
coming back to me, and her kindness, for the first time,
feeling like an achievement. There she was,
cooking our meals, running the house,
my ill mother barely able to assist.
And there was her secret, pressing in
on her and down, asking for release.

That she was impregnated by her teacher at age fifteen,
that the teacher married her and on the wedding night
disappeared forever, that she gave the baby to a relative
to raise, that she'd been sent away—not over—
to America, where she converted shame into silence,
married again, becoming a bigamist, that her husband
and daughter and my brother and I never knew,

   all this speaks to the awkwardness of exposition
and of a concealment so gifted
it's impossible to know the degree
to which it also was tragic—a life denied,
a child left behind. As family secrets go,

   nothing for the tabloids, no one
beaten senseless, or murdered in bed.
But for me things to walk off, and toward,

   about which two dogs from the house
atop Gravel Hill had something to say.
Protective of what they hardly understood,
they charged, barked—good dogs, really,
their tails giving them away, and I turned,
started back, the secret seeming less and less
mine, part landscape now,
part the words used in its behalf.

   A man in a pickup drove by,
his two raised fingers signaling, what?
That unlikely comrades were possible
in this world? That we share a code?
But he'd come so suspiciously
out of the narrative blue.

   If you meet the Buddha on the road,
kill him, Buddhists say, worried
about anyone bearing indispensable news.

Lucky for the man that he didn't stop,
I might have had to eliminate him.
Instead, something grandmotherly—
it must have been grandmotherly—
insisted I just let him be a man
making his way home.
Open a door for him, said that something,
now close it so he's safe within.

I descended the hill,
the dogs still yapping as if certain
they were the cause. Up ahead,
the sudden sun through the trees
had speckled my driveway,
and, at its end, where gravel gives way
to macadam, there was the circle

that allows things
to be dropped off at the front door.
It was all shadowy and clear,
and moving toward it I felt
the odd, muted pleasure that comes
when you realize you've only just begun
to know how you feel.

Brief Answers to Unspoken Questions: An Interview

STYLE. It's like a doctor wishing to have a bedside manner. If it sounds rehearsed, it has been. Some writers think they can will it. When that happens, every effort feels like effort.

No, I don't think the writing teacher in this respect is much different from the physician: the person under examination would like it if we could keep our private lives out of our diagnoses.

A poet of domestic life? Seems rather reductive to me, even though domestic life is an enormous subject, especially if you believe, as I do, it has its mysteries. But to unearth things is not enough. You need to find a choreography for them. The detritus of a day, e.g.—not unlike imagining those creatures making their way toward us in *Night of the Living Dead*, slowly, awkwardly. Opportunities for movement, for undreamed of sympathies.

This is what I know about teaching: If you kiss a gorgeous student, you're likely to kiss another. I've always tried to kiss someone else.

What a good question. I agree, to listen well is an act of curiosity and respect. It presumes that someone has something to say. But I know it's not enough to be a good listener. The best listener listens, à la Wallace Stevens, "with the innermost ear of the mind." Then what he says in response must reflect the quality of his hearing.

I'll answer you this way. My favorite dog cartoon is this one: Two dogs meet on the street, and one says to the other, "They always call me good dog. They never say great dog."

Well, here's what I used to hold dear. A truth is most comfortably received when preceded by an indefinite article—*a* instead of *the* unlocks the noun, makes the truth feel credibly small. Now I think that to make assertions using indefinite articles mostly serves to keep us from making fools of ourselves, and yet, sometimes, don't we have to risk making fools of ourselves? Aren't the most memorable statements asserted boldly, like, for example, Flannery O'Connor's, "The truth will make you odd," or André Gide's, "It is with noble sentiments that bad literature gets written"? Actually, there are many things other than truth that are dear to me. The tone with which something is said, for one. My fear is Stendhal's: ". . . I may have expressed only a sigh when I thought I was stating the truth."

The lesson of Scheherazade: The king doesn't need a reason to fuck me. He needs a good reason, however, not to execute me. Every reader is a potential tyrant. Make sure the page gets turned.

No, you misunderstand me. A fiction is a beautiful thing. It's unmediated and untransformed experience that is a form of ugliness. It sprawls. You can see its underwear.

Hero is the wrong word. I'd say I've often been a protagonist; that is, someone on the verge of learning what everyone else knows about him.

Well, you have to be careful with what you say to certain students. I said to one young man, "You can't go around comparing the yearnings of vampires with your own criminal desires. You're a guy, not a genre; there's less expected of you." He didn't think that was funny, which worried me.

I know what you mean when you say that occasional mischief always seems more interesting than earnestness of any duration. But what if I were to say that there are issues of design and scope to consider, of how and where things fit, not to mention the indulgences of mischief, the poignancies of something actually meant. Oh, I see, I'm proving your point.

No, I loved those writers who addressed my daily sense of dislocation. Beckett and Cervantes and Kafka—those serious comedians. Then, later, Roethke. Rilke. James Wright. The list is long. I used to read to be introduced to myself, and to otherness; I used to read in order to feel normal. Now I'm more likely to read in order to see how a writer got from one place to another, to try to locate the secrets and magic of how something gets made.

Good taste? Nothing narrows what we're able to see and invent more than good taste. Then again, I have to say I've enjoyed many such a narrowing.

Sure, I usually find myself rearranging what I've started. I'm fond of those good bad movies in which tornadoes rip through trailer parks, lives and furniture strewn about. I'm the mayor who tells the reporter, it's time to rebuild, who's fascinated by the odd jigsaw puzzle logic of how things might be put together again. Of course, the stakes become different if, say, my aunt lived in one of those trailers. Lament complicates reconstruction, as it should. I might not want to improve that broken rocking chair, which was hers. Lament just might want me to leave it there next to her son's one shoe and overturned, yet intact tricycle.

Special effects? I hate them. It's the fault of *Star Wars*, a good movie. After *Star Wars*, lots of dazzle, things somersaulting at terrible speeds. Fewer and fewer depictions of people destroying their lives normally. I hate fireworks. I hate parades. Give me backroom betrayals, or a quiet lie that makes a family cascade downward, or through unlikely courage transcend its fate. I never have a good time on the Fourth of July. I refuse to wave to anyone riding in an open car.

Here's something that I'd say to writers: At least have the decency to claim your unhappiness. Don't leave it lying around the house, bleeding like that. Make something of it.

Yes, yes, but sometimes the soul is so sick it isn't able to open the door.

What I mean to say is that my soul stays shy when it hears someone spill the beans.

My influences? Claire's knee. Things half seen. The impossible shot. The need to make my life appear more interesting. More interesting than what? I come with a magnifying glass to the ant farm.

Oh yes, I've had many plans. But "everyone has a plan until you hit them," said Mike Tyson. Careful now, don't automatically discredit what the discredited have said. One punch from him in his prime, and the last chapter of your memoir would need to be rethought. That is, if you were still capable of thinking. When the verdict is in, I often ask myself, how do we keep on going?

I'm so tired of defending atheism. The burden, of course, is on the believers. Me, I believe in love at first sight more than in the existence of God. I believe that if you call someone and she answers she's there.

Really, the obfuscators are cowards. So what if language can only approximate. Some writers approximate better than others. Count me as someone who tries to be as clear as I can about what it feels like to be alive while knowing the heart itself resides in the dark.

Your question is unanswerable. Go away now. I mean I'm not inclined to answer it. Ask me again after five o'clock.

Oh, there are all kinds of great sentences. Joyce's, "A frowsy whore with black straw sailor hat askew came glazily in the day along the quay towards Mr. Bloom" is one of them. "There was an old woman who lived in a shoe" is another. And then there's Mussolini in 1934 saying "We have buried the putrid corpse of liberty," a reprehensible well-turned phrase. Compare it with Eisenhower authorizing the Normandy invasion in 1944: "Okay, let's go." Context raising simplicity to eloquence.

No, I'm a hedgehog *and* a fox. Sometimes I see the world through a single lens. Sometimes the world overwhelms and brims over. I need to widen my glance as often as I need to narrow it. I love Tolstoy. I love Dostoyevsky. Vast and contradictory, let the fun begin.

If you're wondering why I've agreed to your random yet intense questioning, I'll remind you to look up the definition of self-indulgence.

We are responsible for what we invent; God's loneliness is ours. That's my latest position. From now on, when it comes to God talk, I plan to be merciless.

I'll tell you a pretty story, maybe then you'll understand.

There, there, I often tell myself, no weeping. There's still time to revise.

Acknowledgments

American Poetry Review: "Little Craft Manifesto"

The Georgia Review: "Forms and Structures," "Refuge, and the Serious Humor of Kafka and Beckett," "One Summer," "Constructions," "A State of Disunion" (formerly titled "Poetry Now, and Some Thoughts on History, As If, and No"), "Brief Answers to Unspoken Questions: An Interview"

Graywolf Anthology: "Degrees of Fidelity"

Lyric: "The Poem, Its Buried Subject, and the Revisionist Reader"

Plume: "George Orwell Sucks"

"Mr. Flood's Party" was published in *Touchstones*, edited by Robert Pack & Jay Parini (University of New England Press).

"Locker Room Talk" was published in *Short Takes*, edited by Judith Kitchen (W.W. Norton).

"Introduction to *E.E. Cummings' Complete Poems*" was published by W.W. Norton.

"Forms & Structures" was delivered as a lecture at Pratt University.

"Play & Seriousness" was delivered as the Keynote Address at The National Council of Teachers of English in Minneapolis (2015).

"Style" was delivered as a lecture at The Bear River Conference in Michigan (2015).

About the Author

STEPHEN DUNN is the author of over twenty books of poetry and prose, including *Different Hours*, winner of the 2001 Pulitzer Prize. His *Loosestrife* was a finalist for the National Book Critics Circle Award. Among his many other awards are an Academy Award in Literature from the American Academy of Arts and Letters, The Paterson Prize for Sustained Literary Achievement, fellowships from the Guggenheim and Rockefeller Foundations, three National Endowment for the Arts Fellowships, the Levinson Prize from *Poetry*, and the James Wright Prize from *Poetry Northwest*. Forthcoming from W.W. Norton in 2019 is *Pagan Virtues*, a book of poems. He is Distinguished Professor emeritus at Richard Stockton University, from which he holds an honorary doctorate. He lives in Frostburg, Maryland with his wife Barbara Hurd.

Colophon

Degrees of Fidelity by Stephen Dunn was designed by Philip Memmer
using Adobe Caslon Pro for text, and for the cover, Perpetua.
Manufacturing was by Bookmobile in Minneapolis, Minnesota.

This book was published with the generous support
of the following individuals:

James Anderson
Laure-Anne Bosselaar
George Drew
Richard Foerster
Lee Hope
Gerard LaFemina
In Memory of Paul MacAulay
Karla Linn Merrifield
Sterling Watson